Thank you so
much for your
support!

Daniel Faucett

FIVE FLAMING ARROWS

DANIEL FAUCETT

FAUCETT JOURNAL

Faucett Journal
www.faucettjournal.com

ISBN-10: 1546537716
ISBN-13: 978-1546537717

Although the author has made every effort to ensure that the information in this book was correct at press time, the author does not assume and hereby disclaim any liability to any party for any loss, damage, or disruption caused by errors or omissions, whether such errors or omissions result from negligence, accident, or any other cause. Any internet addresses (websites, blogs, etc.) in this book are offered as a resource. They are not intended in any way to be or imply an endorsement by Daniel Faucett, nor does he vouch for the content of these sites and numbers for the life of this book.

DEDICATION

To all the young campers from Teepee #12 in the Summer of 2016. Your passion for sanctification has changed my life forever. I hope this book changes yours.

CONTENTS

ACKNOWLEDGMENTS

Special thanks to Reed Chambers, Joseph Faucett, John Faucett, Anne Faucett, Evan Hatton, & Pastor Jeff Underwood for reviewing my work. Your efforts have been the driving force behind the quality of this book. Without your input, this book never would have become anything more than the twenty-page eBook it started out to be. As far as grammar is concerned, I want to especially thank Suzie Howle for her attention to detail. Any mistakes that remain are my own final editorial mistakes. I also want to thank my wife, Bailey, for creating the cover artwork, various illustrations, and for supporting me in all of my wild endeavors. Your unwavering support and patience have given me the strength to follow my dreams.

INTRODUCTION

In the Fall semester of 2015, I was confronted by a good friend of mine named Todd Kirk. He told me about a summer camp that he worked at in the past, and that I should seriously consider working there. I thought about how I wanted to spend my summer doing my own thing, and living my own adventure. *Why would I want to spend my summer serving others?* I asked myself, along with the important question: *what's in it for me?*

My friend was very persistent, however, in advising me that I needed to work at this camp. He said that it would change my life. I had my doubts that working at this camp would be a "life-changing" experience, but he wouldn't take *no* for an answer. So, around October, I visited The University of Alabama in Tuscaloosa for an interview with one of the camp's directors.

We met at the local student Starbucks—let me interject here and tell you that I hate reiterating the coffee and Christian stereotype, but unfortunately there is a lot of truth to it—and upon arrival I sat down at the first open booth I could find. I observed the commotion around me. There were many other students from all over Alabama being interviewed by people with laptops, coffee, smiles, and Bibles. The interviewees were answering questions about homosexuality, death, the gospel of Jesus Christ, and other key issues that would be important for any counselor to know who would be seeking a job at a Christian sports camp.

Before it was my turn to brave the interview, I couldn't help but think to myself that I wouldn't get hired. I wasn't perfect, but these other people sounded like they were. I was living under the misguided assumption that these Christian camps must be hiring perfect people, and I was not a part of such a category—if there even was one. Nevertheless, it came time for me to take the place of another interviewed student who seemed to be slightly embarrassed. *This isn't going to be good,* I thought to myself as I sat down with the smiling interviewer.

We had a cordial greeting, and the interviewer took a swig

of some hot coffee as he scrolled on the touchpad of his Apple laptop from across the table.

He asked me different theological and doctrinal questions about the Bible right off the bat. (I didn't answer them very well.) He even asked me what verses I would share with a potential camper if they wanted to "Get saved." I paused for some time, muttering quite a few *um's*, and other miscellaneous jargon associated with John 3:16—ultimately I was rambling.

He eventually let me off the hook and said, "I understand how hard it is to answer these types of questions when you're put on the spot." He then told me to study the Romans road to salvation, and that it would equip me for sharing the gospel at camp if I was to be hired. He prayed over me and told me he'd keep in touch.

The interview only lasted a few minutes, but being in the presence of what was clearly a spiritual giant, and someone who had dedicated his life to the scriptures and missionary work, made me feel small, unknowledgeable, and insignificant. However, he was not demeaning or rude when I was displaying myself as a lukewarm Christian. He was very polite, and rightfully questioning whether or not I should watch over twelve kids every week for the upcoming summer. He was personally engaging, and clearly wanted to know my intentions for wanting to work with kids.

I left that interview with the assertion that I would not be hired. I knew that after sharing my testimony, and my imperfections, that they wouldn't hire me. With so many people who had been interviewed, I thought they surely wouldn't pick me out of the crowd. Those other guys were answering questions with appropriate scripture references; they didn't hesitate; they were confident, and they seemed to have less sinful testimonies.

After about two months, in December of 2015, I got an email from the camp's headquarters that I had been hired for the summer of 2016. I didn't know what to think at first. I was excited, scared, happy, and nervous all at the same time. I especially was anxious about how I would make the twelve-hour drive to the campgrounds without a cell phone. Nevertheless, God had given me an opportunity, and I was not going to waste it because of my fear of getting lost. After all, my mother always said, "Don't miss your opportunities." I didn't plan on missing this one.

I eventually made the trip to the campground by using an old cell phone that didn't have a plan or data. I used wireless internet access at various McDonald's to reset my app's coordinates on my generic phone. The GPS signal would die every two or three hours, but would work perfectly again once I reset the coordinates at another McDonald's. It was a sketchy system to say the least, but it worked, and it got me to the greatest summer camp on Earth.

At this camp, I was hired on to the position of counselor for a certain teepee, specifically Teepee #12. Most of the kids that came to this particular teepee were between the ages of thirteen and sixteen. And for my counselor position, I would work alongside another counselor to watch over and minister to a new group of teenagers every week. At the end of each week, the old campers would leave, and new campers would come.

During each week, the friendships and bonds that were made between campers and counselors were some of the greatest friendships ever made. Personally, I became great friends with so many kids, other staff (such as counselors, office workers, maintenance workers, ministers), and many kids' parents. It was an amazing relationship-building experience; something that I will take with me for eternity.

On the first night of each week, my fellow counselor and I always made it a habit for us to share our testimonies with the kids in our teepee. This started each week off with vulnerability, genuineness, and openness—we held nothing back. We wanted to show the kids that we were not afraid to talk about our testimonies, no matter how ugly they were. We wanted to demonstrate that there is no shame in sharing your scars and wounds, because every scar represents a healing from God, and every wound represents an area of opportunity for Him to do more healing.

5

The next night of the week we had campfire night—which has a reputation at camp for being the night when kids open up and confess what is really going on in their lives. After a full day of playing traditional land sports, shooting arrows, water polo, and skiing, we sat down by this fire and got serious. During these campfires, we let the kids do the talking, as compared to night one when we (the counselors) did most of it.

At first, no one would say anything for about five minutes. The awkward silence would build, and the elephant in the room would stomp louder and louder until a camper would feel confident enough—or in desperation to end the silence—to share their story.

It was disheartening to hear the amount of hurt that these kids were experiencing. To be so young, and to have so many battles going on in their lives.

We see kids and we just assume that their lives are easy. We assume this because they don't have the responsibilities that we have as adults; however, they can still be going through the toughest years of their lives when they are in middle and high school. These are the years of everyone's life when they struggle to fit in, find out who they are, and what they are going to do for a career. There are so many unanswered questions, external pressures, and spiritual attacks targeted at teens. Mainly because the Devil knows that if he can kill or prevent someone from forming faith in the teen years he knows he will have groomed them for a lifetime of bondage in sin. For this reason, I think teenagers are probably the most heavily attacked age group.

At least half of the campers each week expressed their battle with pornography or lust. They often said they knew it was wrong, but they couldn't stop viewing it—even though they wanted to quit. If the students were not struggling with lust, then they were struggling with what they had been learning about in their freshman Biology classes.

At least two or three campers each week said they felt like science disproved and/or contradicted the Bible. They said that there was too much evidence. This "evidence" caused them to lose their faith, or at least wrestle with it. Many doubted whether or not God even existed.

Some of the students—a far smaller demographic– struggling with depression. While suicide specifically ʳ much of a struggle or topic of conversation in my ⁺ heard it was in others.

I don't blame any of these campers for s these issues. They are all products and victims their parents and ancestors have created. W blame this generation for their problems, wʰ degree, we should also look at how we havⁿᵉ adults, and how our parents and their pₐ things. What type of environment have we created? When it comes to pornography, it is on the backs of the parents from the start of 1855—when the first pornographic daguerreotype was produced—forward who have allowed pornography to become legalized, mainstreamed, and to establish spiritual strongholds in human hearts. It is the parents of this generation who have made a spiritually dead environment for these kids to grow up in. So, how can we solely blame these kids for only responding to their environment?

I know that they could have chosen not to view certain images, but teenagers already have enough problems of their own. One of the major roles we play as adults is to protect children from these kinds of evils.

We could talk all day about how things should be, but it doesn't look like things will change for a long time when it comes to the negative environment we have created for this generation. So, we have to acknowledge the reality that our world today is broken, a product of sin, and in desperate need of Jesus.

These five areas (lust, the reality that bad things happen, ce, anxiety, and depression) are the five most prominent I saw students struggling with at camp. I couldn't just sit nd watch so many kids struggle without giving them a ething to help. So, besides the counseling that I gave rs that summer, I want to give them this book. I have written this book for four core reasons:

1. To make students and parents aware of these issues.
2. To provide students and parents with a biblical perspective on these issues.
3. To provide mental constructs to help with recovery in any one of these five areas.
4. To make everyone aware of the saving power of Jesus Christ.

Ephesians 6:16 says, "In addition to all this, take up the shield of faith, with which you can extinguish all the flaming arrows of the evil one" (NIV). This verse is the foundation by which my entire book rests. We need faith in Christ (the shield of faith) to be able to truly defend ourselves from the damage that the Devil causes through these five areas.

Furthermore, I think it's about time we wake up and address the detrimental reality we are facing. It is my view that not talking about lust only makes it gain a greater stronghold. Not talking about why bad things happen from a biblical perspective only makes our kids bitter towards God. Not talking about science only reinforces the misconceptions that the Bible is inaccurate. Not sitting down and discussing what the Bible says about anxiety and depression only leaves our kids in more darkness and confusion. When we don't talk about these issues, they get worse. So let's talk.

Daniel Faucett

FLAMING ARROW #1

LUST

Daniel Faucett

1

A SOCIETY OF MONSTERS

I once asked myself the important question: Who is it that influences people's lives the most? My initial thought on the topic was that friends or teachers impact people's lives the most. Nevertheless, in order to settle my curiosity, I sent out a Twitter survey that asked that very question. The answer choices were: (1) a teacher/coach, (2) parents, (3) a famous person, and (4) a friend. 39% responded with their parents, 33% said a teacher/coach, 28% said a friend, and 0% said that a famous person had impacted their life the most.[11]

This is not a reliable piece of research, in fact, I would not even call it research. This is merely an anecdotal dip in a sea of opinions about who is the most influential person in people's lives. It's worth mentioning because parents do, in my opinion, play the most important role in people's lives. And this survey seems to reiterate this view.

However, what's interesting about this survey is that the majority of people felt that their parents have impacted their life the most. Now, of course, this doesn't mean that their parents have impacted or changed their life for the better, it just means they feel their parents have impacted their life the most. Which, depending on the parents, could be a bad thing or a very good thing.

Either way, this should make you consider what kind of person you want to be one day. Especially if you think in terms of the butterfly effect. That everything you do today, no matter how small, will affect someone else down the road. Whether you do something good or bad.

To further illustrate this idea, I want you to think about a time in your life when you lost your temper. Perhaps someone pulled out in front of you, and you had to slam on your brakes to prevent an accident. After you restored to your regular speed, you proceeded to yell out curse words and other anger-driven jargon towards the culprit. Before you knew it, you were steaming with anger, disappointed, and unbearably upset—it ruined your day. This type of incident has done something to that little thing inside of yourself we call your *soul*.

It's this thing we call a soul that is damaged by spiritual abuses. By giving into the temptations of anger or revenge, we damage our already poor soul because we allow it to indulge in something evil. Once we taste an evil, we build up an appetite for it. And before we are aware of it, we have an addiction we can't readily get rid of.

Now, how does this relate to the Twitter survey? Think about this: If you damage your soul today, then you will damage someone else's tomorrow. Unfortunately, that someone else may happen to be your future son or daughter. And, being a parent, you will play the most impactful role in their lives. You will be even more influential than their favorite celebrity, politician, friend, teacher, or coach. It is the little things that we give into today that may negatively affect those that we love tomorrow. This is why it is so important to start down a path right now that will make you a good father, or a good mother, in the future.

Of course, it all depends on what it is you define as a good father, or a good mother. I think if we got five people in a room from various socioeconomic, religious, and cultural backgrounds, we would get five very different answers to that sort of question. Of course, I would take a Christian viewpoint on the matter, and I would give my two cents about how Jesus Christ is the only source of spiritual guidance that can influence a man, or a woman, to become a good father or a good mother. A good parent is simply someone who obeys Christ first, serves others second, puts himself third, and sacrifices his personal desires daily for the glory of Jesus. However, not everyone will buy into this truth. I know I would be right to make such a statement, as you will see that the Christian Bible is a superior and supernatural document; however, the head knowledge of Christ doesn't help us any if we don't allow Him to invade our lives and change our hearts. Unfortunately, some of you will quit listening to what I have to say simply because I have taken a stand on Christ as my source of strength in such a matter.

However, I think everyone can agree, whether you are a Muslim, an atheist, a Christian, or a Buddhist, that what we do today matters. That our actions can affect other people down the road. And from a spiritual standpoint, the things you do today especially affects that little guy inside of ourselves we call our soul. And that our actions may lead someone to—or away from—the Cross. Since all of our actions shape who we are, who we will become, and our potential as a vessel for Christ to use, every action has eternal significance. With every little episode of abuse, over indulgence, anger, lust, or disrespect, we damage our soul. We become people who lead others away from the Cross. Over long lengths of time, repetitions, and indulgences, we become an unrecognizable monster.

If you know anything about monsters, you know they are

not easily controlled. At some point, they always hurt someone else, even if in the moment the monster seems like a beautiful angel. That is the thing about monsters, sometimes you don't recognize them for what they are until they have already taken your well-being, reputation, or even your life.

This is why we should pray when we are faced with a situation that is tempting. Indulging in our natural inclinations is usually sinful and detrimental, even though we may see it as harmless. Our actions, in physical and spiritual reality, will inevitably deal damage to someone else down the road.

Take, for instance, a fictional character named Chad. Chad is a teenager who loves basketball. He trains every day in the gym. He is also a Christian who enjoys reading His Bible. However, Chad has a weakness. Whenever Chad is confronted by his parents for missing curfew because he was at the gym, or for making a bad test grade, he keeps his mouth shut until he can get to his room, where he then curses his parents under his breath in a fit of uncontrolled anger. Chad has never repented from these intense private outbursts. He has never tried to make things right with his parents afterwards because he feels that as long as they don't know he's angry, then there is nothing wrong with his episodes. He certainly has never prayed for forgiveness from his anger, and He has never tried to change.

Fast-forward fifteen years. Chad is a lawyer in New York,

City, married to a kind woman, and has four kids. He has the perfect life from an outside perspective. However, his anger problem is even worse now. It has grown and grown over the years into something unrecognizable. Whenever his wife doesn't have supper ready, it's an outburst of anger. Whenever the kids leave their toys in the living room, it's an episode of verbal abuse that leaves them crying and emotionally damaged. His anger has become a driving force of his behavior—a controlling influence.

The repercussions of his anger tantrums have negatively affected his relationship with his wife (who would leave him if it were not for their four kids), and with his kids (who do not enjoy spending time with him because he pops off at their slightest misbehavior). Why has Chad let his anger get this bad? At some point, he must have realized he was losing control of his anger, and that it was becoming a dominant influence in his life. Where did it all go wrong?

It all went wrong when he was in high school. When he was a young ball player consumed with what he thought was a little, insignificant sin that didn't really matter because he kept it to himself. On the contrary, the little sins become big sins over time. What he thought was little then, has now grown into a tree of hate and anger that has separated himself from his wife and kids. He often feels guilty about his episodes, but he doesn't know how to change, or to prevent them from happening in the future.

You may think this situation seems unlikely, or perhaps even unreasonable. You may be thinking that most people are rational, and that they will recognize their problems and change via the processes of social, mental, emotional, and physical development accompanied by self-actualization. You may be right to say that in some cases. But I would argue that those are the vast minority of cases. True growth can only come when a plant has good soil and is watered regularly. Most people, however, turn themselves away from the Good Soil and the source of Water. They know they need help, but they turn to things that can't help them.

This is why we see adults behaving so irrationally; they are separated from the Good Soil and Water that is Jesus Christ. This is why we see adults have red-faced and curse-filled temper tantrums when their order is incorrect at a fast-food restaurant. This is also why we, as adults, with fully developed brains, ignore the reality that if we cheat on our wife, we will face the utmost of consequences. We would think that humans are rational beings, but on the contrary, we are infinitely irrational. We raise our irrationality to whatever level is required to justify our actions, and this is due to our separation from Jesus Christ—the only Being that can make us truly rational; or, at least, rational in the sense that we know right from wrong, and that we have a source of strength to stay on the right path.

But back to the main dish: that what we do today matters. C.S. Lewis once said in *Mere Christianity* that, "Good and evil both increase at compound interest. That is why the little decisions you and I make every day are of such infinite importance."[10] To make it even more clear, let me explain compound interest. Essentially, if you invested 1,000 dollars with a 5% interest rate, and you left it for ten years, after one decade it would be worth 1,629 dollars. Comparatively, with simple interest, it would only be worth 1,500 dollars. You see, with compound interest, every year the interest rate is applied to the new value. So every year the growth of your money is bigger and bigger.

I believe our soul works the same way. When we invest in evil, it compounds on itself and grows even more worse than we would have expected. But the same goes for when we invest in Christ. Our spiritual growth is even better than we would have expected it to be. So, this is why the little things we do today are so important; they compound on themselves to make us monsters, or they compound on themselves to make us disciples of Christ. Each path will affect the eternal destination of ourselves and those around us.

Of course, I believe it is a spiritual revelation to come to the acknowledgement that what you do today matters. It is the Holy Spirit that gives us a sense of urgency to repent. These are qualities given from God because He can see how our actions today will affect others in the future. That is why Christians throughout the centuries have tried to get this message across. It is why they have been able to forgive so quickly, even in the face of the utmost of offenses. It is not that Christians have some amazing willpower on their own, but it is the supreme power of Jesus Christ that brings them to their knees to confess their sins, to repent from them, and to turn back towards God.

If you remember one thing from this book, please remember this: It is never the wrong time to turn to Christ.

The issue is that our fictional character, Chad, did not take the opportunity to repent when the sin was less dominant in his life. If Chad would have repented from his sin of anger when his parents first started to drill him about his grades and curfew, then God could have shaped him into a man of love before he ever became a father of anger—before he ever became a husband of anger.

And that's the real issue: Husbands are *supposed* to represent Jesus Christ and His covenant with the church by the way they treat their wives. Through service and sacrifice is how this covenant is represented, as you will see later. But for Chad, it is hard for him to make sacrifices or serve his family today because he is consumed with a sin that controls his life.

I'm not saying that God can't change Chad now. God is all-powerful; however, what I will say is this: it takes time to change. It takes years of passionate dedication to the scriptures, to prayer, and to cultivating a relationship with God through Jesus Christ to experience plentiful, spiritual growth. While God can change you immediately, what I have noticed, in my life and others, is a gradual growth. And since it seems more often than not to be gradual growth, why not start that process as soon as possible? Why wait until your sin is out of control?

You must forgive me, I don't want to bash anger too much. After all, I do believe you can be angry and not sin. For example, Jesus Himself displayed anger when turning over the tables of the money changers in the temple. But this anger was pure in its intent, not out of anger against a sinner, but out of reverence for God and anger against sin. However, disrespectful and hate-filled anger that is directed towards a person (and not their sin) is an example of a sin that can become a controlling influence in our lives. And in Chad's case, it did just that.

I encourage you to repent from your sin today. If you do not repent, at some point that sin will control your behavior, ruin your marriage, or even your ability to be a good father. That is not what God wants for you. He wants to break you free from your chains. Whether that be chains of anger, unforgiveness, doubt, lust, gluttony, or bitterness. You have to repent from your sins, and be actively seeking Christ to develop in you what He wants to develop, which is the fruit of His Spirit. We all want to be a dad or a mom that can love our kids with the love of Christ. But in order to do that, we have to allow Christ to be number one in our hearts. Above anger, above lust, and above any other sin that can capture us and train us to be monsters.

As you will see in later chapters, lust is just a mechanism that the Devil uses to keep you away from our good Father. My hope, as a result of you reading this book, is that you will come to realize the importance of pursuing a life that is more concerned with giving God glory, than it is concerned with trying to feed a monster of sin that is controlling your life.

And since we are on the topic of monsters, I think it is appropriate to quote a great friend of mine. In an article published on Faucett Journal, Brad Easley (2017) once compared the darkness of our sin to the fear of monsters under the bed:

Without light, we are blind as bats and fearful as children who aren't quite sure whether there's a monster under the bed or not, and the older we get, the more comfortable we get with the monsters, the more we make friends with them, the more we become numb to their abuse, and eventually, we too ourselves become the monster under the bed for someone else. (para. 1)[9]

The little indulgences today slowly make us monsters in the future. It is not that we instantly become monsters, but through many repetitions, indulgences, and time spent living in sin.

The path to become a monster is similar to the track of sanctification, only the road is paved in the opposite direction. In sanctification we develop the fruit of the Spirit. To do this we have to have repetitions in reading God's Word and praying to Him. We have to *indulge* in Jesus. In the path to become a monster we also need repetitions and indulgences. Usually these are simply falling into that particular sin time and time again until we lose all control and we become slaves to it. However, both paths take a lot of time. It will probably be at the end of your life when you realize what you have truly become—a monster or a disciple.

The issue today is that we have created a society of monsters in many areas, especially the area of lust. Kids are getting introduced and addicted to pornography and premarital sex at young ages. By the time they are developed into parents, they are grotesque monsters. These two evils, pornography and premarital sex, are preparing people to be very unfaithful, unloving, and monstrous parents. And what's most unfortunate about this reality is that they will have the greatest impact on their kids' lives.

2

SEX AND MARRIAGE

Let me start by saying that I am no theologian, not by any means. There are many people out there who know a lot more about the topics of marriage and sex and their purposes than I do. I can only give you my thoughts on the topics. Nevertheless, I will try to evaluate them appropriately, and when I may have over casted myself with respect to them, I will try to reel in closer so that I do not fall off the boat.

First, it is important that we establish what it is, as we discussed a moment earlier, that is making people monsters. In my opinion, it is the indulgence in two spiritual evils: premarital sex and pornography. These two sins are so indulged in by our society that over time people become sexually handicapped and grotesque monsters that hurt other people.

If we do not understand why marriage—and sex in the context of it—is sacred, then there would be no reason for us to avoid these two spiritual evils. There would be no reason to avoid pornography or to practice abstinence. And most importantly, there would be no reason to treat women like our sisters in Christ. What you will notice about everything I talk about in this chapter is that it all rests on the foundation that is the sacredness of Christian marriage.

Defining Christian Marriage

In Christianity, marriage is symbolic; that is why God takes it so seriously. You see, marriage in Christianity represents the covenant between God and man through His Son, Jesus. Marriage is a symbol, or a reminder, of spiritual truth. Ephesians 5:22-23 tells us, "Wives, submit to your own husbands, as to the Lord. For the husband is the head of the wife even as Christ is the head of the church, his body, and is himself its Savior" (ESV). So, in a Christian marriage, according to Ephesians, the husband represents Jesus, and the wife represents the body of believers. When you really sit down and think about the appropriateness of these two representations, there is no other symbolic representation of marriage that makes theological sense.

If God (whether you believe in the God of the Christian Bible or not is irrelevant to this hypothetical proposition) in some form does exist, then you would expect purpose behind His creation—or, at least, the major institutions. So, if marriage is an institution made by a sovereign God, then what symbolism from the major religions makes the most sense?

Let's take Islam. In this religion, Allah has no son. Therefore, there is no absolute guarantee of salvation, nor is there a genuine relationship with God. The relationship between man (who is inherently sinful), and Allah, cannot be bridged because Islam does not guarantee forgiveness of sins through a blameless sacrifice. So, what does marriage in Islam represent? It is hard to say. In Christianity, we have a clear correlation between what we see in objective reality and what we can reason theologically about the Son and His relationship with the body of believers. In Islam, however, the spiritual symbolism does not adequately represent a relationship with God—it is disconnected and does not fit objective reality and what we experience.

You would think that if Islam were true, that marriage (the climax of human intimacy) would accurately represent some spiritual intimacy portrayed in the religion. But with this religion it is disconnected. My conclusion is that Christian marriage is the most appropriate marriage. Not because

Christian marriage looks any different than any other marriages (although it should), but because the objective reality of marriage only makes sense in light of the Christian symbolism for marriage outlined in Ephesians 5:22-23.

In objective reality we experience marriage as deeply intimate and spiritual—euphoric even. So when Ephesians tells us that the husband is a reflection of Christ, and the wife is a reflection of the body of believers, it makes perfect sense. Christ is so in love with the body of believers that He laid down His life for it. We get such an overwhelming sense of love in our earthly marriages that we are willing to lay down our life for our wife's wellbeing. My conclusion is that the objective reality of marriage—passionate love, joy and sacrifice—is truly represented best by this biblical analogy.

Unfortunately, some people have used this analogy to control women. They see the analogy made between Jesus and the Church and immediately think about obedience and control. While obedience is a component (because the husband should be the spiritual leader of the home), focusing solely on it merely drags the discussion away from what's really important about this passage.

These verses are talking about *real* leadership, and a real leader leads by example. Take Jesus, while He possessed the authority being Himself God in the flesh to simply tell His disciples how to live a life that glorified God; instead, He also lived out a perfect example for us to follow. Of course, we should teach the Word to our family, but it shouldn't end there. Men are not merely teachers and leaders of the home. We must also lead by example, through service and sacrifice, which is the example that Christ set for us thousands of years ago. Jesus said in Mark 10:45, "For even the Son of Man came not to be served but to serve, and to give his life as a ransom for many" (ESV). The two recurring themes of His earthly life: service and sacrifice. We see them over and over in His words and in His actions. We, as husbands, must strive to be a reflection of these two spiritual qualities in our homes.

A real leader does not make trivial requests to reassert his authority. And if you think about it, why would someone filled with the Holy Spirit want to boss their wife around just for the sake of being a boss? If anything, we should desire to serve our wife more than they serve us. If we can do something for ourselves, then we should do it for ourselves. If we can do something for our wife, then we should do it for them without hesitation. Our service for our wife should be so quick and automatic that it seems like we are merely serving ourselves. In fact, it may feel like you are serving yourself in some respects because your wife is a part of your own flesh. Ephesians 5:28-29 says, "For no one ever hated his own flesh, but nourishes and cherishes it, just as Christ does the church, because we are members of his body" (ESV). We cherish our wife because she is a part of our self, and we naturally cherish our self. Needless to say, this heightened level of service (above what is normally seen in marriage) reveals that we care about Christ more than it reveals that we care about our wife. And that is the exact example that we should desire to set for our children and to those who may not believe in Him.

Ephesians 5:25 goes on to explain how sacrifice is also a component of Christian marriage, "Husbands, love your wives, as Christ loved the church and gave himself up for her" (ESV). We truly exhibit love for something when we are willing to give things up for it. For instance, if you really loved basketball, then you should be willing to make sacrifices for the sport. You should be willing to give up your money, your weekends, and your afternoons, all for your progression in the sport. Similarly, with marriage, if you really love your wife, you should be willing to make sacrifices for her. You should be willing to make sacrifices of your time and money. However, in both cases, you should *want* to make those sacrifices if you truly love what it is you are making the sacrifices for. But in the case of marriage, the most predominant way a man shows love for his wife and family is through sacrifice. The man must sacrifice his time in order to work hard to provide for his family. The man must sacrifice his own desires in order to provide for his wife and children. This sacrifice is ultimately a picture of Christ's sacrifice for us. When you think of marriage in light of this sacrifice, it points back to the Cross. And once again, we find that the objective reality of marriage (that the husband shows his love for his wife through sacrifice) fits the symbolism posed through the institution of Christian marriage.

Life After Marriage

But focusing in more detail on marriage, I think it is also relevant to mention sex. While of course, you can have sex without a marriage, it is still important to focus on the possible symbolism of sex in the context of a Christian marriage. You see, the wedding ceremony, as we mentioned earlier, represents the moment that Christ comes back for the church (the body of believers), but what does the life *after* this ceremony represent, and why is sex so pleasurable?

For one, the life after marriage represents our relationship with Christ once He returns. When Jesus Christ returns for His church, at the end of time, we will be in the presence of our Lord and Savior face-to-face. Of course, we are in constant communication with Him now; however, our relationship currently is inhibited by sin. In contrast, upon our Savior's return, we will finally have a relationship with God that is uninhibited by sin. Likewise, in our earthly marriage, we are in a constant and uninhibited relationship with our wife. When you're dating, however, you're constantly having to manage each other's schedules in order to spend time with each other face-to-face. It is inconvenient, tiring and annoying. In contrast, when you finally become married, your relationship with each other is uninhibited because you now get to live with each other. You get to enjoy all the pleasures of a constant, face-to-face and intimate relationship. There is nothing that comes between you like there used to be when you were only dating. Of course, sin is still a huge problem after you're married even if you both are saved, but the barriers of time, space, and residence that were once hindering your closeness have now been removed.

But why is sex so pleasurable? What about sex could be spiritually symbolic? In order to answer these questions, I must quote my college ministry friend, Aaron Walker. He once said, "I believe God made sex so pleasurable to give us a taste of how amazing life with Him face-to-face will be." If you think about it, sex is probably the most enjoyable and pleasurable physical act you will ever take part in on this earth; therefore, it should probably represent the most enjoyable and pleasurable spiritual state. Therefore, sex most likely is symbolic of a face-to-face relationship with our Savior. Can you even imagine the euphoria of living with the One who died for your sins face-to-face? It will be the most joyous, amazing, and pleasurable experience of our entire existence. Furthermore, I believe that this future face-to-face relationship with Jesus will surpass anything we have ever experienced on this earth—including sex, which has been called the climax of the human experience.

I believe that the reason the Devil wants to destroy our respect for sex in the context of marriage is because sex represents this future face-to-face relationship with our Creator. If the Devil can get us to disregard the Lord's design for sex in this respect, then he can keep us from experiencing joy with our future wife. The Devil has been incredibly successful in this mission; according to Jayson (2006), "Of those interviewed in 2002, 95% reported they had had premarital sex; 93% said they did so by age 30."[7]

I think if we focus on what sex represents—our future intimacy with our Creator—then we might be better able to resist our desires to indulge in premarital sex. The issue is that we don't see sex as something sacred and designed. We see it as simply a pleasure. We have glorified it in a purely physical sense, almost as we have with food and technology. We have opened it and exposed it as nothing more than a product—and in our own country, a product you can purchase.

Five Flaming Arrows

3

ABSTINENCE

Now that we are aware of why marriage is so sacred, and why sex in the context of it is also, we can begin to understand why we should abstain from sex until marriage. There are four main reasons why I believe you should practice abstinence:

1. Marriage is sacred
2. Abstinence develops self-control
3. Abstinence develops patience
4. Abstinence protects us

We should abstain from sex until marriage because marriage is a sacred covenant. It is a covenant under God between the husband and wife, which is a representation of the greater covenant between God and man through Jesus Christ—as we talked about earlier. With this biblical understanding in mind, it changes our view of marriage and sex from pleasure and status to grace and genuine love.

I think, though, that when you talk to teenagers about sex, they have a hard time seeing it in this manner. They are so enculturated that they see sex as simply a pleasurable way to bond with someone you like. However, when you see sex the way God sees sex (a holy covenant and representation of His own personal love for us), it changes the way you view abstinence. Abstinence is no longer seen as a rule to be followed, but a goal to be achieved in order to honor our Lord.

Self-Control

We should abstain from sex until marriage because God uses our journey of abstinence to develop in us two virtues: patience and self-control. Self-control is simply the ability to control your actions. Every person I know has a different degree of this virtue. Some of my friends succumb to the slightest temptation, others I know can withstand the strongest of temptations. Some can work jobs that they hate, others can't work at all. My brother, David, probably has the strongest level of self-control I have ever seen. He has lived in the poorest of conditions, lived off the cheapest of foods, often rode his bike to work (even in winter); he has never missed a day of work regardless of how he was feeling; he was a straight A student at Auburn, and can resist anything offered to him if he thinks he shouldn't take it. It's not just that David was born this way, but that over time he developed this virtue.

When David was a homeschooled youngster, he worked for our dad in the yard (which was no easy task). He built all kinds of machines, and fixed almost anything our family needed fixed. By the time he became a teenager, he immediately started working at Hardee's, and worked there throughout high school. In college, he found other jobs to stay alive and sustain himself until he was able to finish school. David has worked hard in every stage of his life, and through this he has developed self-control and a hard work ethic.

When it comes to abstinence from sex, it works the same way. Abstaining from sex until marriage develops self-control in our hearts. Whenever we are tempted by something, and then because of our convictions we abstain from giving into that temptation, we immediately become a more empowered person—we immediately have more self-control. It's not that God doesn't want us to experience pleasure, but it's that God wants His followers to have extreme levels of self-control for the future trials we will face.

Any good father should have his children do chores in order to develop their work ethic. Dads know that their children will have to work hard one day in order to provide for their future families. So, it's not that the father wants to force his kids to do work for no reason, but because he wants to help them. He wants them to become men who can provide for their future wife and kids. One of the chores, so to speak, that God gives us to develop self-control, is the challenging process of abstaining from sex until marriage. It is through this process that we slowly become men and women who can be faithful in the future.

If we do not develop self-control while waiting until marriage, then we will not be prepared to be faithful to our future spouse. What will happen when we are faced with the temptation to cheat on our spouse? If we have not already allowed our Lord to give us the strength to resist before marriage, then we will be too weak to resist the temptations of another woman after marriage. God knows that our actions today will affect us down the road, that is why He wants us to develop this virtue as soon as possible.

Furthermore, I think it helps in the development of our self-control if we consider the eternal nature of our existence. If we do have an eternal mindset, when we are married and we are tempted to pursue intimacy[12] with another woman, then at that time we should consider that our time on earth is a small fraction of our existence. If we are truly believers, and we understand that we have eternity to get to know all other believers, then why are we not willing to wait to get to know another believing woman when we get to eternity? In truth, most adulterous relationships are not caused by lust, but by the building of a true and genuine friendship. It's these true and genuine friendships with other believing women, that often arise within the church, that we should be wary of when we are married. I think it helps to have the mindset that you can simply wait to get to know them deeply when you get to eternity.

Of course, we shouldn't long for deep friendships with other women. If we are longing for intimacy with other believing women then I think we have another problem altogether. Longing for intimacy with other believing women is an indicator that your marriage is not going so well. Additionally, this longing is dangerous and puts your marriage at risk. Fortunately, I think this eternal mindset concerning relationships helps us put our social interactions and desires into the right perspective.

All believers are children of God, and one day we will all be reunited into immense intimacy. It is at that time that we can be free to develop closeness with everyone—even other women—because the danger of adultery will be gone because it will no longer exist. But right now, the stakes are too high. Our covenant marriages are too important.

This mindset is healthy in reference to all relationships between believers. There are many people I can think of today, who I no longer know as well as I would like, but who I am excited about getting to see again (and getting to know better) in the eternal Kingdom. Many friends from homeschool, middle school, high school and college who I know now to be great workers for the Kingdom, who have moved away and become distant, or who have died at young ages. These people I will get to know deeply in eternity, and it gives me peace to know that this small earthly existence is not the only time I will have to pursue intimacy with them.

Of course, anyone, whether secular or Christian, can develop self-control through abstaining from sex—they do not have to have an eternal mindset or the Holy Spirit. However, through Christ, God helps us gain a level of self-control beyond what we are physically capable of achieving through our own effort. This is because self-control, according to Galatians 5:22-23, is a fruit of the Holy Spirit. If we have a relationship with Jesus Christ, and we are diligently pursuing purity while waiting until marriage, the Holy Spirit is operating in the perfect climate to develop in a Christian a superior level of self-control. And if you think that Christians do not have a superior level of self-control, I would encourage you to read *Tortured for Christ* by Richard Wurmbrand. In this book you will find Christians facing some of the most intense tortures and persecutions, yet they still joyously glorify God and serve others. At one point, one torturer in the communist prison became a prisoner next to the Christians he had once tortured. The Christians who had been most tortured by this man were the very ones who protected him from the other prisoners who wanted revenge. They even gave him their own rations. Therefore, I believe there is a worldly self-control that we all can develop, but I also believe there is a God-given self-control that is superior.

This God-given self-control affects every area of our lives. Just like we learned in chapter one, that the little things we do today are so important because they compound on themselves; they bleed over into every crevice of our hearts. You could call it the *Theory of Connectivity*: that everything you do is connected to, and affects, everything else you do in the future. Everything you think today will affect the way you act tomorrow. It's like our lives are composed of an endless array of connections, cause and effect relationships, and since God is all-knowing, He is well aware of this system. I think that is why we see such strong expressions about self-control in His Word, because God knows that self-control is so deeply at the root of this web.

According to Proverbs 25:28, "A man without self-control is like a city broken into and left without walls." (ESV). If you do not develop self-control, then you will have no guard against the temptations of the Devil in the future. You will have no "walls." That is why it is so important to start asking

God to give you self-control today, because without it you will be very vulnerable when the Devil attacks you later in life.

To further explain this idea, I want you to imagine yourself walking in the parking lot of a convenient store. You notice a fifty-dollar bill that was likely dropped by the gentleman ahead of you fumbling with his wallet. You have two options: you could take the money, or you could bring it back to the gentleman. If you take the money, you could justify the action because, after all, it may not have been his. Or, you could grab the fifty-dollar bill and return it to the gentleman, regardless of whether you know it was his or not. Truly, you should return it to him simply because you desire a pure conscience, and you know that having to wrestle with that discrepancy over the next few days would hurt your spirit.

This seemingly trivial act of self-control in the area of finance will carry over into how you treat your wife when you get home. Do you give her the benefit of the doubt when you think she has misplaced something of yours? Do you show her love, and help her accomplish all the things that she wants to accomplish? Simply because you desire to have a clean heart when you close your doors and talk to God at night. Not that you think you are perfect, but that you try your best to be like Jesus and have a clear conscience.

Everything seems unrelated at first glance, such as with self-control in the area of lust, our future relationships, and the way we act in every other area of our life today. However, in reality, everything is interrelated because every action we do comes from our heart. And only a heart that seeks Jesus Christ, and His dominance over itself, will blossom in all areas.

Patience

In addition to self-control, we also develop patience when abstaining from sex until marriage. This patience that we can develop through this process is superior to patience developed through alternative or worldly means. God knows that through this process of abstinence He will be able to make us more faithful husbands and wives in the future. He will be able to make us more patient as well. And, most importantly, He will make us more reflective of His Son—who displayed supernatural patience. So, if you can lean on the Lord to grow patience in you to abstain from sex now, then you will be a more patient spouse in the future when you actually get married (as we mentioned earlier, self-control works the same way).

If you want to be a rocket scientist one day, then you should start preparing right now, even though you are only a student. You need to study the necessary background subjects, such as aerodynamics and physics, in order to prepare yourself for success in the future. If you want to be a patient husband, then you need to ask God to make you a patient son, friend, and boyfriend right now. You don't just wake up one day as a patient husband, and you don't just wake up one day as a rocket scientist, both take years of preparation. The only difference is that genuine patience is developed ultimately by our Father's divine intervention in our lives, and through our intense dedication to His discipline.

God's discipline is good because it shows that He loves us. If He did not discipline us or give us guidelines, then how would we know that He cared for us? It's through His discipline and intervention in the things we do—every aspect, including sex—that reveals how much He cares about our lives. If you think about it, the worst thing that a parent can do to their children is not discipline them or be involved in their character development. That is probably the most hateful thing because it shows that they do not care how their children turn out.

Thankfully, our heavenly Father cares. So much so that He is involved in every aspect of our lives with His divine discipline, especially in the area of sex. He gives us guidelines concerning our sexuality because He wants to discipline us. He wants to develop in us virtues and character so that we may become more like His Son.

Abstinence Protects Us

Building on this idea that God cares for us, we should also

abstain from sex until marriage because God's guidelines for sexuality are there to protect us. To establish this point, I want you to imagine a suburban home. Where there are two loving parents and two young children. The children—a boy and a girl—like to spend their time after school riding their bikes in the yard. However, there is a road nearby where cars tend to drive very fast. The parents, knowing this dangerous fact, tell their kids that they are not allowed to wander into the street. They tell their children that they may only ride their bikes in the yard. Why do the parents give these guidelines? It's not to keep their children from experiencing pleasure, but because the parents want to protect their children from harm. The parents know that one day the children will be able to experience the road, but that day is for the future, when they are older and mature enough to navigate the road safely.

To God, we are merely children riding bicycles. God gives us guidelines in many areas because He wants to protect us, especially in the area of sexuality. Just like good parents don't allow their children to wander into dangerous streets, God does not want us to wonder into some of the dangerous situations that come from having premarital sex. However, the harm that God is protecting us from is twofold: emotional and spiritual.

By commanding us to wait until marriage to have sex, He is protecting us emotionally because we must wait until we are truly committed before we take part in the super emotional stimulus that is sex.

I had a very wise co-counselor, Will Garza, who worked with me in Teepee #12 at camp for a few weeks. He once told me, "Sex will make a relationship that should not last long, last a very long time." I think Will was right. Sex causes people to become extremely emotionally attached. When it is premarital, it causes two people who may not want to commit to each other to stay together for the sole purpose of an unwarranted emotional and physical addiction. If those two people are not compatible, for instance, if they disagree about politics, religion, and have conflicting personalities, then those people may stay together simply because of the emotional attachment that results from having sex. Over time, maybe even after three or four years, when the emotional high and physical attraction settles down, the two may split up. Then, they may start another physical relationship with someone else that keeps them in a dark connection for another three or four years.

God, with his guidelines for sex, is protecting us from this vicious cycle. He wants us to be absolutely sure that we want to spend the rest of our lives with someone before we ever have sex with them. He knows that sex can cloud our vision, and has placed guidelines for our sexuality in order to protect us from this cloud. Unfortunately, we are not so wise as to listen to the Lord's instruction. We like to veer into dangerous circumstances before we are mature enough to navigate them safely.

God's guidelines for sex are there to protect us while we mature. So that one day we can navigate the dangerous roads. God wants to teach us patience and self-control—which are two gifts cultivated by His Spirit—in order for us to mature spiritually. He teaches us this patience and self-control by helping us abstain from sex until marriage. In order to abstain from sex, we must lean on God constantly and seek His face above our fleshly desires. This process leads to spiritual maturity. God wants us to mature spiritually in this manner before we ever get married, because He wants us to be mature enough to navigate marriage and sex safely.

When we try to participate in marriage and sex before we experience some level of spiritual maturity, we are most likely walking into a disaster. We may experience an emotional and physical addiction with someone that we are not meant to be with, or perhaps, we will simply degrade our values to the point that we are not prepared to spend the rest of our lives with one person.

Additionally, premarital sex with multiple partners may lead to STDs, stress, guilt, and/or unexpected pregnancies. God doesn't want us to live like that. He wants us to be spiritually strong men and women who get married and committed before they ever participate in sex. This results in people who are mature enough to navigate sex safely—which would be participating in sex only in the context of marriage.

4

EPIDEMIC

As we discussed earlier, there are many reasons to practice abstinence. Most importantly, we develop two virtues: patience and self-control. Now, in this chapter, I would like to take the discussion a step further and talk about something that is even more ignored by our society than sex—the issue of pornography. This problem, having been ignored, has grown into its own tangled issue. It's kind of like a box of electrical power cords. After a long period of time the cords start to become more and more tangled. Eventually, the cords get so tangled that it becomes an excruciating endeavor to untangle them. This is the situation we are in today with pornography. It is so pervasive, so tangled up, that it will take many people working diligently to straighten it out. Here are some jaw-dropping statistics on the issue of pornography; I think they will reveal to you the condition of this box of tangled cords:

- According to a survey by the Barna Group in the United States (2014), "64% of self-identified Christian men and 15% of self-identified Christian women view pornography at least once a month (compared to 65% of non-Christian men and 30% of non-Christian women)."[4]

- Every second, 28,258 people view pornography on the internet (Ropelato, 2007).[2]

- According to Ropelato (2007), "The pornography industry is larger than the revenues of the top technology companies combined: Microsoft, Google, Amazon, eBay, Yahoo!, Apple, Netflix, and EarthLink."[2]

- Also, according to Ropelato (2007), "Every 39 minutes; a new pornographic video is being created in the United States."[2]

- China's porn industry revenue is around 27.40 billion dollars ("Pornography Statistics," 2006). This is enough money to feed 62% of the world's hungry for a full year.[3]

- South Korea, whose porn industry revenue is around
  25.73 billion dollars, is enough to feed 58% of the
  world's hungry for an entire year ("Pornography
  Statistics," 2006).[3]

My initial thoughts on these statistics was that the world is in a
state of crisis. Just look at the last two statistics alone; if China
and South Korea quit spending money on pornography for a
year, they could use those funds to end world hunger, and even
have a 20% surplus at the end of the year which could be used
to dig wells in Africa.

What these statistics show is that our actions have
consequences. People suffer because of the sinful indulgences
of others.

When you think about it in a spiritual sense, this issue's
prevalence reveals a glimpse of the spiritual world and its
impact on our own. The fact that there is no self-control in this
area of people's lives, accompanied by the fact that people are
acting so irrationally to perpetuate this epidemic, reveals that
this is a spiritual problem. Why else would people buy into
something so detrimental if it were not somewhat spiritual? I
know there are physiological components to this issue, but at
their most basic form they are still spiritual. Even though you
allow yourself to become physically addicted to a stimulus, the
giving into that stimulus is a spiritual problem at its most basic
form. (There is a duality.) To put it another way, perhaps

someone is a pathological liar, having spent his whole life lying, his physiological structure would be altered in a way that encourages lying—whether dopamine is released, or some mental circuits are stimulated. However, that person still has a choice on whether or not to fall into that particular sin. It is quite possible that their physiological structure makes it harder for them to resist lying, but that doesn't mean they can't resist. And, once again, it is a spiritual, free-will issue at its most basic form.

One question that non-religious people often ask is this: "Is pornography really such a bad thing? After all, they're not hurting anyone." I know it may seem like a legitimate question, especially from a secular point of view, but in reality it is extremely misguided. To be blunt, I think the only reason people ask this question is because they are more concerned with pleasure than they are actual truth. You don't have to look very far down the rabbit hole to find the plethora of problems that arise from a worldwide pornography epidemic (such as people are starving while others are viewing it, and its impact on divorce).

One argument I often hear, from the more libertarian-minded individuals at least, is that pornography is a non-issue, and if people want to produce it and watch it, then they should have the right to do so; so long as it doesn't negatively affect, exploit, or hinder the rights of other people. However, is it not obvious that pornography negatively effects and exploits the people viewing it? It negatively affects not only the viewers, but the producers, "actors," and every person who meets a viewer.

Let me explain what I mean: Strong families are the foundation to any prosperous and free society. There is no structure that better guides families than the Word of God. What pornography has done, is it has infiltrated the family, especially fathers and sons, and has caused these men to devalue what scripture says about sex. This has caused the majority of American fathers to seek sex outside of their marriages, and sons to fall into premarital sex. According to Kevin B. Skinner (2011), "In a 2004 testimony before the United States Senate, Dr. Jill Manning shared . . . that 56% of divorce cases involved one party having an obsessive interest in pornographic websites."[1] This reveals that out of the one million divorces every decade, over half of these could be due to pornography addictions (Skinner, 2011).[1] This problem is nothing short of an epidemic, and it's killing families while we ignore it.

This is where the lie of pornography—that it doesn't affect others negatively—is ultimately exposed. Imagine the broken families, the children who will never be tucked in at night by both parents. All because someone felt that their gratification was more important than their family's wellbeing. A father is risking everything by indulging in pornography, especially in regards to his relationship with his wife. But even more important than that, as we discussed earlier, marriage is sacred because it represents the covenant between Jesus and the church. Thus, to put that relationship at risk is to threaten everything Christianity stands for.

But how does a pornography addiction affect young men? It programs them to see women as nothing more than subordinated, sexual objects. Women are made in the image of the living God. They should be treated and valued as such. However, pornography is training men to subordinate women. It achieves this by lying to them about the reality and value of women.

To explain what I mean further, think about this analogy: Watching pornography is synonymous with listening to lies about the physical world around you. Imagine if you spent time each day listening to someone talk about how the world is flat. At first, your knowledge of the world, and your ability to critically think would override the incoming stimulus of lies. However, over time, you would eventually begin to meditate on those lies, thus internalizing them. Eventually, this exposure would change the way you see the world. You might even start to believe the lie. Likewise, by viewing pornography, people are constantly being fed lies that women are less valuable than men, and that their only purpose is sexual gratification.

Eventually, men see women differently, they see them as merely sexual objects, which could not be farther from objective and spiritual reality.

It's not that pornography has instant ramifications—while it does have them—but it's mainly the prolonged effects that are much more serious. Such as the inability to build a *real* relationship with a member of the opposite sex; or, the catastrophic effect of a later-in-life-acquired addiction that eventually destroys a relationship that was already built.

Lecrae Moore, the talented rap artist who received a Grammy Award for Best Gospel Album, co-founded Reach Records, and is a world renown hip hop artist and record producer, details his sexual experience as a child in his book *Unashamed.* He reveals that he had been exposed to sex as a young child; after which, he became sexually "rewired" (Moore, 2016).[6] Sex and pornographic imagery affects the brain in that it causes people—especially young children—who are exposed to it to see women differently. It's like revealing a veil with cookies behind it to a kid, once they see it, they want it. When it comes to Lecrae, he said that he was just mimicking what he had been exposed to. When you are exposed to something this intense, especially at such a young age, it can have detrimental effects to your brain. Unfortunately, the average age of exposure to pornography is eleven years old (Ropelato, 2007).[2] Are we so foolish to believe that the daily indulgence of pornographic images by our kids isn't rewiring their brains as they develop into young men?

For the rest of this chapter, I will focus primarily on why pornography is such a bad thing. I understand that the topics I'm about to talk about are very unpopular, and may even be awkward. But I think that shedding light on certain topics usually is awkward, so we shouldn't let that stop us from addressing pornography.

If you have already heard a detailed explanation of these topics, then you are free to skip to the next chapter. I hope that you will choose to read them anyway, though, as a means of re-oiling the gears of your mind. The topics I will cover are these:

- Pornography Shrinks our Hearts
- Porn teaches us to justify our sin and avoid confession
- Porn teaches us to devalue scripture
- Your body is a temple
- Porn is unloving
- Kids need to be kids
- Porn alters the mind

Pornography Shrinks Our Hearts

I am a firm believer that a heart after God grows towards God. Not that we can do this on our own effort, but through the influence of the Holy Spirit we can grow towards God when our heart has been set after Him. However, our heart only gets set after Him by His influence, so neither I nor anyone else who has experienced His grace has a right to boast. Therefore, we grow towards God because our hearts find satisfaction in Him. Consequently, when we set our heart and mind on pornography and seek satisfaction from that, our heart shrinks towards our flesh.

Paul tells us in Romans 8:7-8, "For the mind that is set on the flesh is hostile to God, for it does not submit to God's law; indeed, it cannot. Those who are in the flesh cannot please God." Imagine the small, hard, and pathetic heart that must arise from years of pornography indulgence. Years of setting your mind, heart, and soul on sexual gratification of our flesh. When we set our heart's desire on something like this on a daily basis, it results in a hard, compromising, and unrepentant heart. A heart that literally cannot please God.

It would be the same case if someone made it their life goal to become financially successful. Their heart would shrink down to that desire. They would, at the end of that journey, come out on the other end a very unpleasant and compromising person who values financial success over everything else.

On the other hand is a heart set after God. Paul goes on to say in verse nine, "You, however, are not in the flesh but in the

Spirit, if in fact the Spirit of God dwells in you." (ESV). In this case, when we have the Spirit, our heart grows towards God—rather than shrinking down to a dishonorable passion. But, like verse nine tells us, this comes about only when we are in the Spirit (which is what happens when we have been invaded by Christ). When we have His Spirit in us, we want to do whatever it takes to give Him maximum glory—which means we must *minimize* our own. Doing away with our foolish desires and pursuing His will at all costs.

I think the contrast between setting our minds on the flesh, and setting our minds on Christ, reveals the obvious need for Christ. Especially in recovery from a pornography addiction. If we set our minds on porn, our hearts will only reach the level of our goal. However, when our goal is Christ, our life becomes a pursuance of His glory. This pursuance results in spiritual development and fulfillment.

Porn Teaches Us to Justify Our Sin and Avoid Confession

When we try to justify an addiction because we think we can't live without it, or because we think it's not wrong, it can lead us down a very scary road of sin justification. For instance, many people justify a pornography addiction because they believe it is a mood-boosting, non-addictive, and stress relieving act. However, punching a coworker you don't like in the face may also be a mood-boosting, stress-relieving, non-addictive act; nonetheless, that doesn't mean that that action will not carry consequences. The same goes with pornography, there are many detrimental consequences that come from viewing it. Whether you *think* it is a beneficial act is not relevant. The consequences of viewing it are prominent and unavoidable.

When we take part in a sin so often that it becomes a part of our daily routine, it becomes increasingly difficult to separate ourselves from the act. The result: we justify the act. We tell ourselves very silly things like, "we are just guys," or "it's only natural." But let's be honest with each other, sin is natural; and we are all aware of the natural power of sin. Almost every experience in our life is affected by it. Yet, we still try to use the excuse that "sin is natural" to justify our actions. We cannot use the naturalist approach to sin justification without acknowledging that we are lying to ourselves, yet people use the natural excuse all the time. While sexual desire is a natural craving, similar to a hunger for food, it should only be satisfied in the context of marriage—as defined in the Bible. Anything outside of that context is sin, and we are very silly liars to think that we can justify our sins with excuses and get away with it without consequences.

Additionally, porn teaches us to avoid confession. You see, when you are addicted to any sin, it causes shame and internal turmoil in your conscience. The specific sin you struggle with is not as important as the underlying issue: you have put something before God. Deep down, you know that this placement is wrong. That is why being addicted to those things can cause you to avoid confession of your sin: you are simply ashamed of yourself.

Porn Teaches Us to Devalue Scripture

When someone gives into pornography continually, it reveals a heart that is either ignorant of scripture or one that has devalued it. For instance, the Bible takes marriage extremely seriously. So much so, that the only way you can be free from a marital bond is through death, or through sexual immorality (see Mathew 5:32). We are also commanded not to defile the marriage bed by having sex before marriage (see Hebrews 13:4). Not only do we have these guidelines, but Paul reveals to us in his letter to the Ephesians that marriage is a reflection of the covenant between Jesus Christ and believers (see Ephesians 5:22-33). Therefore, my conclusion is this: If you are indulging in pornography, you have either devalued what scripture says about marriage and sex, or you are ignorant of it.

To be ignorant means that you lack knowledge in a particular area. When it comes to pornography, it makes sense that some people take part in it because they are unaware of how God feels about it. If they became aware, by reading this book perhaps, then maybe they would change their ways. If they did not change their ways after they were made aware of God's words, then they have officially devalued scripture. (Of course, I believe everyone has the knowledge of the Law within themselves, as I think C.S. Lewis makes quite clear in *Mere Christianity*; hence, everyone has devalued scripture).

But to the one who—more consciously—has devalued scripture: you are much worse off because, eventually, you will devalue any and all scripture that challenges you. At first, you may only devalue what the Bible says about purity and the holiness of marriage because those are the verses that contradict your *current* desires. However, after you are married, perhaps you will devalue what the Bible says about adultery, faithfulness, and loyalty, simply because you want to have an affair. Then, before you know it, you have completely devalued everything scripture says about Godly relationships.

What's next?

You will begin to devalue scripture in other areas of your life. Perhaps the areas where scripture restricts you from receiving the immediate pleasure that you want. Perhaps you will want a brand-new car in the future; in order to satisfy this pleasure, you will take out a loan (knowing that scripture discourages going into debt).

It's not that we are such monsters immediately (although

we really are), but it's through years of devaluing scripture in various areas, and indulging in sin, that we become a really grotesque one.

Your Body is a Temple

Another truth to consider is the sacredness of your body. Think about it, you have been made in the image of God. Genesis 1:27 reveals this truth to us, and Paul reveals a deeper understanding of the sacredness of the human body in 2nd Corinthians 6:16, "For we are the temple of the living God" (NASB). We are *all* made in the image of God, even people who never accept Jesus Christ; however, only those who are saved by Jesus have the Holy Spirit living in their hearts. Therefore, only those who are saved are a temple that God's Holy Spirit dwells in (see 1st Corinthians 6:19-20).

If you are a human being, then the sheer fact that you are made in God's image should cause you to think about how God sees you. God looks down on you and recognizes that you are more than an animal—spiritually and mentally—and much more valuable (see Mathew 10:31). He genuinely cares for you, and wants you to come to repentance (2nd Peter 3:9). If you are reading this book, then He has given you the resources to become aware of these facts. You must, at the very least, acknowledge these spiritual truths and appreciate them. I don't think it would be too out of line to suggest that these truths encourage those who are not followers of Jesus to consider how they treat their bodies.

More so, if you are saved, and you are a temple of the Holy Spirit, then you should appreciate that God dwells inside of your heart and has taken residence there. He has made us a temple by His presence; we should treat our bodies accordingly. You wouldn't put pornographic imagery on the walls of a church; likewise, you shouldn't put pornographic imagery in the walls of your heart. When you think about it, it's really the same thing. You, as a Christian, are the church. You are a part of the body of believers.

According to 2nd Corinthians 6:15, Paul challenges us by asking us, "What accord has Christ with Belial?" (ESV). In other words, Christ and the Devil have no unity, they are completely separate and opposite. Christ is holy, perfect, and blameless; while the Devil is evil, perverted, and deceitful. You, in Christ, are seen as holy by God. Not because you are holy in any way on your own, but because Christ has covered you with His redemptive blood. Blood that He shed on the Cross thousands of years ago. So, we should ask ourselves, "What unity (or accord, or agreement) do we have with pornography and lust?" The answer is none, because we have been separated from those things through Christ. Just like Christ has no part in those things, neither do we. Therefore, we should acknowledge this truth, change the way we treat our bodies, and filter what we allow our bodies to see.

Porn is Unloving

The issue with lust, like all sins, is that it grows bigger and bigger and eventually gets out of control, like a fire. And while it starts in your own yard, it will eventually make its way into someone else's. That "someone else" will likely be your future wife. In other words, the sins that burn you today, will burn the people you love tomorrow. And your future wife deserves to have a man who can be faithful to her. If you are addicted to lust, then you will be unprepared to be faithful, and that is one of the most unloving things you could possibly do to her.

No woman should have to worry about her husband's faithfulness. But in order for you to be a man that your future wife doesn't worry about, you need to develop a record of trustworthiness. One that shows her that you will only pursue sexual satisfaction from your future wife. If you live a life in pursuance of Christ, then your wife will be able to trust you when you finally do get married, because you will have a record of character and obedience to Christ. When you do get married, the logical conclusion is that this character and obedience will carry over throughout your life. It will increase your ability to be faithful to your wife.

Do you ever wonder why Christians put so much trust in God? And why we trust what His Word says? It's because God has a perfect record. He has always kept His promises, and He has fulfilled His prophecies—especially the prophecies about the coming Messiah. For instance, Psalm 22:12-18 describes the crucifixion of the coming Messiah. It turns out that Jesus Christ miraculously fulfilled this prophecy (along with Isaiah 53). However, what's amazing about the passage in Psalm 22 is that crucifixion had not yet been invented when it was written. How did the writer of Psalm 22 articulate crucifixion before it was ever invented? It is because God is interweaving time and space for His glory, and prophecy is one avenue by which He accomplishes this goal (as you will see in much more detail later in this book).

However, we as Christians believe in God because of His record of supernaturally fulfilled prophecy, His perfect record of keeping promises, and because of His investment in our lives. This consistency and record of God is something we, as Christians, should pursue. Not that we should attempt to make new prophecies, or try to play God, but that we should seek to be consistent and trustworthy. That we should seek to keep our promises. For instance, we should pursue obedience and consistency in the area of purity. This results in a reputation of trustworthiness that our future wife rightfully will demand.

Our wife needs us to have a consistent history of pursuing purity. If we have a bad record, then when we get married it will be even harder to build trust. However, if we have pursued purity already, our wife will understand our history, and they will rightfully trust us. Of course, this principle goes both ways. Men also need women who have had a record of pursuing righteousness and purity.

You need to start asking God to make you that man now. Don't wait until you are married to be a man after God. Ask Him to make you that man today. A man who desperately seeks to manifest the fruit of His Spirit. Who has a biblical outlook on life. Who sees everything through a biblical lens. Who values scripture over culture. Who sees the sinful world as redeemable. Who asks God to free himself from the grips of lust. Who seeks sanctification, and a deeper and more intimate relationship with the Father through Jesus Christ. If you pursue that relationship with God, then all the aspects of being a *real* man will manifest themselves in you, and you will be able to truly love your future wife with the love of Christ.

Kids Need to be Kids

When I was eleven years old I was homeschooled. And being a homeschooler, of course, meant I went to school at my own house. Therefore, my classmates were my five brothers and my sister Rachel. In the mornings, we learned about science, English, math and the Bible from our parents. In the afternoons, we built forts, played with Lego's, made fires, blew stuff up and fought beetles.

My younger brother, Josh, and I would often get ants from two different ant beds and put them on a barren piece of dirt. We would then watch them fight like they were part of a mythological war. We also would pour ants on the water to see what they would do. They would usually gather into a makeshift boat and sail to shore riding on each other. Once they arrived at shore, they would disperse.

One time we put a wasp in an old peanut butter jar to see if he could make nice with a few ants. They actually all ended up being friends—or at least it seemed like they were friends. They probably lived in a state of mutual fear rather than actual peace, but still, it was an experiment for the books, and we both learned something from it. These odd experiments with insects is where I first found my interest in science. When I do experiments now, I am reminded of these days. (While our experiments probably were unethical, they were very interesting!)

We also lived next to a swamp. Whether it was Summer, Winter, rain or snow, we would still go down to that swamp and build teepees. Some teepees from the older boys were extremely advanced—incorporating insulation and chimneys. For entertainment, we would have mud fights from across swampy creeks. My brother David, who later became a mechanical engineer, built a catapult so he could launch larger mud balls at us. We even had our own currency in this land we called Swamp Town—which at one point consisted of empty glass beer bottles we found on Possum Trot Rd. When Swamp Town progressed into a more developed society, our currency changed into slits of bamboo sticks.

It was the life. I couldn't be more grateful to God for such an amazing childhood. However, the point I want to make is this: Imagine how the innocence of children can be distorted by the early exposure to pornography. Keep in mind that the average age of exposure is eleven years old (Ropelato, 2007).[2] And when they are exposed at such a young age, their goals go from fort-building and mud-throwing to desires that they shouldn't even be thinking about. My heart breaks for the childhood innocence that has been cut short by the epidemic of early exposure to pornography. I believe we must protect our kids by allowing them to *be* kids. Of course, we should explain to them the dangers of pornography, but we should not allow them to be exposed to it—the consequences are too severe.

You wouldn't let your child do meth, smoke a bunch of cigarettes, or drink alcohol, so why would you let your child view pornography? They are all indulgences that have catastrophic consequences. You should not feel like an overbearing parent when you create boundaries for your children that keeps them from accessing pornography. It is ok for you to protect your child from something that can have such negative effects on their well-being.

Porn Alters the Mind

Pornography not only affects yourself and others negatively, but it also alters the human mind. I believe the human mind grows around and becomes accustomed to what it uses to accomplish tasks. It's like a Chinese watermelon company that grows their melons in wooden boxes, resulting in square watermelons. Comparatively, with adolescents who grow up on technology, their mind will grow differently than the minds of people who grow up without technology. These young, technology-infused minds become addicted to technology, and they regularly use it to accomplish tasks. It becomes hardwired into their brains as they develop.

For example, a student who grows up in the 2000's will have grown up on technology. When technology is taken away from that person, it will take him or her a lot of time and effort to reconnect with reality and find a new way to solve problems. Technology has become a crutch in this situation. The watermelon company uses a wooden crate to alter the shape of the melons; the human mind uses technology to accomplish tasks and thus wires its circuits accordingly. Hence, I believe people who view pornography as a means of satisfying their sexual desires—especially from an early age—are training and wiring their brains to be crippled sexually. So, when they finally are in a real relationship that is based on trust, and they want to get married, they will find it increasingly difficult to treasure complete sexual satisfaction in their wife alone. If you don't believe me, just ask anyone who has walked into a marriage with a pornography addiction (if they are willing to admit it).

Their brains at this point have become so hardwired to porn that completely shifting gears takes a miracle. Similarly, as seen with students who grow up on sophisticated tech, those persons will have to expend incredible amounts of time to learn how to solve problems without it. And this is where my analogy breaks down: technology isn't always a bad thing, but pornography indulgence *is* always a bad thing. Using technology to accomplish tasks increases efficiency and leads to a rise in production. However, pornography always has negative effects—spiritually, mentally, and physically—no matter how much you indulge in it.

Physically, pornography plays with a chemical in our brains known as *dopamine*. Dopamine is one of the six primary chemicals that plays a significant role in the brain's sexual stimulation (Carter, 2013).[5] Dopamine is responsible for the rewarding feeling you get when you do something pleasurable. Whether that is using cocaine, methamphetamine, or viewing pornography; this chemical's transmission in the brain is increased. In male rats, we find that they will copulate and become aroused every time a new sexual partner is introduced (this is known as the Coolidge effect). They will do this almost indefinitely until they exhaust themselves. Additionally, each time a new mate is introduced, even behind a screen, the male rat's dopamine transmission will be increased (Fiorino, Coury & Phillips, 1997).[8] Therefore, we can see the evidence for how we could become sexually crippled by pornography indulgence. The dopamine causes us to want to indulge in more and more pornography. According to Carter (2013):

> Because erotic imagery triggers more dopamine than sex with a familiar partner, exposure to pornography leads to "arousal addiction" and teaches the brain to *prefer* [my emphasis] the image and become less satisfied with real-life sexual partners.[5]

This addiction to pornography cripples us sexually because it makes us more interested in internet imagery than in our physical wife.

You can quite easily imagine the problems that this could cause in a marriage. If you *prefer* internet images over your own wife, then your wife will constantly come up short to your preferences. You will constantly compare her to your unrealistic standard, and she will never measure up. You will destroy her confidence because of this. Do you really want to continue in your sin, knowing the effect it will have on your future wife?

5

BREAKING YOUR ADDICTION

There is so much out there on how to break free from an addiction, whether it be cigarettes, alcohol, or even a sex addiction. There are people who dedicate their entire life to learning how to free people from these addictions, and I am so glad that there are people out there doing that for others. However, none of them will give you what your soul is thirsty for. You see, all that the world has to offer are ways in which to make yourself more self-righteous. Ways in which you can empower yourself to overcome X, Y, or Z. I'm not saying this is a bad thing in all cases. For instance, if someone has a stealing problem, I find it very helpful that they can seek help, and be empowered to stop stealing. Or, if someone is addicted to cigarettes, it is beneficial for them to seek help and to be empowered to quit.

Similarly, with a pornography addiction, you could find someone out there who could help you quit via a secular method, and it would benefit you and society. Perhaps you would end up with the same results as a Christian who is helped by a pastor: free from your addiction. But, you must ask yourself this question: What's the difference in a Christian recovery and a secular recovery from an addiction? Physiologically, they are probably exactly the same. Both people no longer view pornography, smoke cigarettes, or drink alcohol. However, the difference between the two journeys to recovery is much different, and very spiritual in nature. It is this spiritual nature of addiction recovery that I believe God is most concerned with. God is more concerned with what the desires of your heart look like at the end of your life than He is the addictions you overcame.

Someone who has recovered from an addiction through the Christian mechanism (i.e. through their relationship with Jesus Christ) will have immense gratitude towards God at the end of that kind of journey. The person who overcomes an addiction because of some secular strategy will probably just see themselves as a good person. This is wrong on two accounts: (1) it is a lie, and (2) you are less likely to seek God after that kind of journey. It's this leaning on God to overcome an addiction that strengthens our relationship with Him. Yes, you can overcome an addiction through secular means; but, remember this, at the end of the day, the important thing is where you are in your relationship with the Creator of the universe. While there are secular systems in place to solve a lust problem (although I'm not aware of any good ones), I know none of them treat the source of the problem, which is your heart.

Take my father, John Faucett, for example. He recently had an issue with his heart; two heavily clogged arteries, one had 90% blockage and the other had 70%. The doctors didn't say, "Well, I guess we better find a cream to put on his skin that may heal his heart." No, they said, "We have to get to the source of the problem, we must get to his heart." Just like these wise doctors, who unfortunately had to saw my father in half, rip out his heart, and sew new veins to bypass the clogged arteries, so too does God get down to the root of our problems. Only God takes it a step further with our heart, instead of bypassing clogged arteries, He gives us a new one.

This is also one reason why we are so reluctant to follow God. We know that He wants to saw us in half spiritually, get to know us completely, and invade our lives with His powerful Spirit. This process is scary, and many of us will never find Him because we are too afraid of the vulnerability that is required of this spiritual surgery.

And it is our heart that is completely depraved and broken. This is why we need to be changed from the inside out. This is why mechanisms of recovery that aim at fixing a person from the "outside in" simply do not work. And if they do, they are a quick-fix method that only works momentarily; eventually they will return to their addiction. Or, they will find a new one. The issue is that these outside-in methods are only treating the symptoms of the problem. In contrast, God's Word offers us a solution that works from the inside out. Just like the wisest doctors on earth treat the source of people's problems directly, not the symptoms.

Obviously, this type of recovery that I am talking about here necessitates a heart-changing experience. An experience that must be greater than all outside-in methods of recovery, otherwise, it wouldn't be worth mentioning. Now, before I explain this transformation of one's self, I must first explain what I am *not* telling you. I am not telling you that this mechanism of recovery should only be sought after to pursue recovery from an addiction. This inside-out method of recovery is much more than that. This is a transformation of one's self that results in a relationship with Someone greater, who saves us from an eternity of weeping and gnashing of teeth. Ultimately, a transformation that brings us into a place— or a standing—with God that cannot be undone.

This transformation, this inside-out metamorphosis, is called salvation by Christians. As we discussed earlier, this salvation is not attained based on our efforts for God, but on God's effort for us. So what we do as Christians is this: We hold on to the promise of salvation that God has revealed to us in His Word.

This is why the Bible is truly incredible, it is full of promises from God. And the common thread throughout, from Genesis to Revelation, is that Jesus Christ has come to save man from his sin—a miraculous promise. For we are inherently dead in our sins, meaning we are completely, spiritually depraved and lifeless from birth. Jesus came and died on the Cross for these sins that make us lifeless, so that we can be given new hearts that make us full of life. This is salvation: A promise from God that all those who confess with their mouth that Jesus is Lord, and believe in their heart that God raised Him from the dead will be saved from their sins. According to Romans 10:10, "For with the heart one believes and is justified, and with the mouth one confesses and is saved." (ESV).

We come as we are to Christ, and then through Christ we experience change. Many people feel that they must change first, and then come to Christ; this is a lie from the Devil himself. Trust me, there is not a Christian that has ever existed that was perfect before they came to know our Lord and Savior Jesus. Everyone born on this Earth, except for Jesus

Christ Himself, is a sinner fully deserving eternal condemnation. You, at your worst moment, are in the most perfect moment to come as you are to Jesus. Then, once you have accepted Jesus Christ as your Lord and Savior, you can start to break free from your addictions for good. Or at least you can break free from your addictions without finding new ones to replace them.

Once you have a new heart, one that has been changed from the inside out by Jesus, then you can truly recognize the root of your addiction. The Bible tells us in Ephesians 6:12, "For our struggle is not against flesh and blood, but against the rulers, against the powers, against the world forces of this darkness, against the spiritual forces of wickedness in the heavenly places" (NASB).

Therefore, our struggle against lust is much more than a mental and physical battle. While Satan manifests himself through physical and mental avenues, the actual battle is going on spiritually. Therefore, the roots of our addiction are demonic in nature. Since Satan and his demonic influences are the "wickedness in the heavenly places," we need to lean on the righteousness in the heavenly places, that is Christ, to overcome the Evil One and our addictions.

Now, simply having a changed heart does not immediately heal us from all our addictions. While I have heard that this is the case for some people, it is most often not the case for believers. We still struggle with the things that we struggled with before we were saved; however, now we have an internal motivation not to give into the temptations that we used to give into so easily. We are now intrinsically motivated to turn away because we have a new Spirit living in us. One that is guiding our every move.

Just like a good general in the field of battle uses tactics and maneuvers to defeat his enemy, so too should we use spiritual tactics to defeat our enemy, the Devil. Here are four spiritual tactics that I believe are essential in the process to recovery from an addiction:

- Accountability
- Prayer
- Boundaries
- Scripture

There is one thing that all four of these tactics have in common: they increase our ability to obey God. The confederate general Robert E. Lee once said, "You cannot be a true man until you learn to obey." I think he was right. Until we learn to obey God, we will be clueless as to how we should lead others. And we may as well learn how to obey by starting with Someone who has never been wrong. It's not that we follow God blindly (while at times we may), but it is that we remember His perfectness, and hope that He continues to be exactly the way He always has been.

Accountability

This brings us to our first tactic in the war of recovery: accountability. This tactic is the most unpopular because it requires you to communicate with another person about your addiction. This is something that requires you to swallow your pride, and allow yourself to be vulnerable. It may seem unnecessary, and it very well may be the case that you can overcome an addiction without it. However, I will say that to avoid this tactic would be unwise and, as you will see in a moment, unbiblical.

However, to be truly held accountable for your actions, you need someone who makes it their mission to hold you accountable. This person is called an *accountability partner*. This is simply someone who holds you accountable for your behavior. It's more like a business deal, or a contract. If the addict ever falls back into their addiction, whether that be alcohol or pornography, then they must contact their accountability partner. Then, he or she can pray for the addict, talk them through it, and encourage them to pick themselves back up. Galatians 6:1 tells us, "Brethren, even if anyone is caught in any trespass, you who are spiritual, restore such a one in a spirit of gentleness" (NASB). We all need someone we can lean on, especially a close friend. While we do have Jesus, and as you will see I believe we must lean on Him too, we must also pursue Christ-centered friendships, both of which are important to our growth as believers.

You do not want to be alone in the process of addiction recovery. You are already in a very hard situation, not letting someone in on your life only makes it even harder. Recovering from an addiction is sort of like building a house, it requires a lot of tools, tactics, *and* people. We need friends, Jesus, prayer, accountability, boundaries, and the scriptures. If we ignore these things, then the house that is our spiritual life will be very weak; or, it will never be built in the first place.

Now, concerning the idea of an accountability partner, whom should you pick to wear that hat in your life? I believe it is very important that this person be deeply invested in Jesus. Someone who has a very good understanding of what scripture says about sex in—and outside of—the context of marriage, and who understands that marriage is a symbol of the covenant between Christ and the church. If they do not understand this, then they do not need to be holding you accountable or giving you advice on this topic.

Also, do not pick someone to be your accountability partner who is failing in this area of their life. Ask someone who has been through this situation, but who has come out on the other side a free man. This is the type of person who knows what the journey is like. They know the roads not to go down, the ones to take, and the ups and downs. They are the ones who can give you good advice because they know what works from experience. How can someone caught in the same addiction help you recover? They have not removed the log from their own eye yet, so how do you expect them to see clearly to remove the spec from yours?

If you were going to be trained by someone in basketball, you wouldn't pick someone who doesn't know anything about the sport. You would pick someone who has mastered the sport, like Steph Curry, Kevin Durant, or Lebron James. Likewise, your accountability partner should represent someone who has overcome an addiction to lust, and who is living righteously in this area. And if Jesus is not at the center of their testimony, don't ask them to help you. Because true triumph is characterized by the replacement of your sin with satisfaction in Jesus, not simply trading your pornography problem for another addiction or sin, such as self-righteousness or pride.

I know I've put a lot of stipulations on what kind of person would make a great accountability partner; so please don't misunderstand me. I'm not telling you that this person has to be perfect. All I'm saying is that you need someone who puts Jesus first, has a biblical understanding of marriage, and who has already overcome the same addiction that you are struggling with.

You may also be wondering, "Why do I need to confess my

sin to someone else, isn't God enough?" Well, God is the only one who can forgive you of your sins. However, James 5:16 tells us, "Therefore, confess your sins to one another, and pray for one another so that you may be healed" (NASB). We need people on this earth to whom we can confess our sins. This helps us heal. Moreover, we are commanded to do this. And it's not that these people are forgiving us of our sins, but their encouragement helps us heal from the brokenness that is in our hearts. It gives us someone that we can talk to about our problems face-to-face. Additionally, it gives God an opportunity to show His grace and mercy through another believer.

Prayer

The second tactic I would like to discuss is prayer. Many times when I pray, I feel like I'm talking to the air. I feel like no one is listening. This is the exact feeling that the Devil wants me to have. The Devil knows the power of prayer, that is why he doesn't want me to do it. That is why he tries his best to discourage you by trying to make you feel silly when you think about praying. The Devil uses the feelings of our hearts to deceive us. Jeremiah 17:9 tells us, "The heart is more deceitful than all else and is desperately sick; who can understand it?" (NASB).

We, in the twenty-first century, are controlled by our heart and its feelings. We even abort babies because we "feel" that they are not humans. Even though we have no real scientific reasoning to back up those feelings. We take a similar approach to prayer. We don't pray, not because we don't believe in prayer, but because we don't feel like it helps. Just because you don't feel like something matters, doesn't mean it doesn't matter. For example, just because you don't feel like gravity is important, doesn't mean that it isn't responsible for holding everything down on the surface of the Earth. Just because you don't feel like God answers prayers, doesn't mean that God hasn't answered millions of prayers throughout man's existence.

First Kings tells us that Elijah was once commanded by God to go to Zarephath to dwell with a widow. When he arrived there, he found this widow in a sad state of poverty. Her condition was so poor that she claimed she and her son were going to die. However, God provided for them by means of a miracle. God made the widow's little jar of oil and jar of flour pour a never-ending amount of substance for them to live on.

Despite this amazing miracle, the family still had more trouble to come. Soon after this, the son of the widow became sick and died. Elijah, in complete desperation, carried the boy to the upper chamber of his bedroom and laid him on the bed. First Kings 17:21-22 tells us:

Then he stretched himself upon the child three times and cried to the Lord, "O Lord my God, let this child's life come into him again." And the Lord listened to the voice of Elijah. And the life of the child came into him again, and he revived. (ESV)

If Elijah did not believe in prayer, then he never would have asked God to revive this boy. Likewise, if we do not believe in prayer, or make an effort to pray, then there is no telling what miracles we are missing out on. Perhaps we are missing out on something incredible.

I can remember one terrible morning when my good friend, Zade Adams, passed out during work with heart complications. When he was finally found, his heart had completely stopped. He was declared dead by the emergency team (cardiac death is what they called it). The paramedics immediately put him in the ambulance and rushed him to the local hospital in Jacksonville. They tried to shock him back to life multiple times on the way there, but it wasn't working. Fortunately, for an unknown reason, Zade's heart started back on its own. If it were not for his heart miraculously starting back on its own, he would have died.

So Zade was alive at this point, but the danger wasn't behind him yet. His chances of surviving were still less than 5%. And if he did survive, his chances of not being brain dead were less than 1%. To say the odds weren't in Zade's favor was an understatement.

When I heard the news of Zade's initial condition, I immediately went into my room and prayed. I prayed harder and more intensely than I had done in a very long time. I could feel the gravity of the situation, so I acted in the only way I knew how. God heard me, and hundreds of others in our community, and He answered our prayers. Just like Elijah prayed to God that He might put life back into the widow's son, so too did we pray for God to put life back into Zade. God answered our prayers; He started Zade's heart back; He literally brought Zade back from the dead. And thankfully, Zade didn't have any brain damage after it was all said and done.

I think the problem for us, though, is that we are too concerned with how we *feel* about prayer. So much so that it keeps us from asking God to do the impossible for us. In this situation, there was no way that we could've brought Zade back to life; nor could we keep him from having brain damage. Of course, there was amazing technology that helped do the job. But, according to the odds (which were practically zero), I have no doubt that God was responsible for his revival. God was responsible for the health of his brain.

When it comes to our own lives, we need to dedicate time to prayer. We need to *believe* in prayer. There is often no way for us to overcome certain obstacles, and it is in these times especially that we should pray to God to overcome them for us.

Concerning addictions, we need a devout prayer life if we are to truly overcome them—especially one as toxic as lust. Whenever you are tempted to give into lust, simply pray to God to take that desire out of your heart. Pray with the passion and faith of Elijah.

But let's be honest with each other, we cannot help but feel the way we feel about prayer. We are not in control of our feelings; however, we are in control of our actions. And we don't have to act the way we feel about prayer. The way we feel about prayer is irrelevant to it being real, intimate, or helpful. So, what should we do with our negative feelings towards prayer? I believe we should ask God to take those desires and feelings out of our hearts. (We will most likely follow our hearts, whether they desire evil or good; this is precisely why it is so important to ask God to change them.)

Specifically, I believe we should ask God to create in us a pure heart, as David did in a verse you are probably familiar with: Psalms 51:10 says, "Create in me a pure heart, O God, and renew a steadfast spirit within me" (NIV). However, I'm guessing there's something about the context of this verse that you are not familiar with: David said these words to God *after* he had already committed adultery with Bathsheba.

Not only should we ask God to purify our hearts so that we

can have the right mindset towards prayer, but we also shouldn't stop praying just because we've messed up in the past. David messed up in one of the worst ways possible: he committed adultery. He destroyed and disregarded a sacred covenant. However, he still sought God afterwards in prayer. He still asked for a pure heart from the Lord.

Unfortunately, most people today do not turn back to God after they mess up. I see it all the time with guys struggling with pornography addictions; they say that since they have already messed up so much, there is no point to even pray anymore. The reality is that these guys are missing the bigger picture. It doesn't matter if you have fallen once, or a million times, God wants you to repent. Second Peter 3:9 tells us that God wishes that none should perish, but that all should come to repentance. So this means that it is never too late for us to turn back to our merciful God in prayer.

Furthermore, Proverbs 4:23 tells us, "Above all else, *guard* [my emphasis] your heart, for everything you do flows from it" (NIV). Every action starts in the heart, whether it be good or bad, obedient or rebellious. Therefore, it is critical—concerning our ability to obey God—that we ask Him to create in us a pure heart. If we can be given a supernaturally pure heart from the Holy Spirit's presence, then the desires of our heart will change. Perhaps we will no longer even desire to fall into the temptations of adultery or pornography, and we will be more suited to obey our Lord. And, since we want to be true men (as defined by Robert E. Lee), then we must pursue a supernatural level of obedience.

Boundaries

Emphasis was put on the word *guard* in my reference to Proverbs 4:23 because I believe we can apply this verse to our physical life. We can do this by using the recovery tactic known as *boundaries*. You see, not only should we ask God to create in us a pure heart, so that our desires can come from Him; but, we must also guard our own hearts with physical boundaries.

For example, many people access pornographic imagery on their smartphones and computers. One way in which to employ the boundaries tactic would be to make rules concerning our access to technology.

Rule number one: you can never bring your smartphone into a private area. Since most people view pornographic imagery when they are alone, this rule will keep them from having the opportunity to access it when they are alone.

Rule number two: laptops should only be used in public rooms in the house. This means that if someone wants to use their laptop to do a school project, they must use it in an area of the house where roommates or family members spend most of their time. This rule holds you accountable because everything you do on that computer is visible to the people in your house. While people are more open about their sin these days, I still do not believe that even the worst scumbag could view porn in front of their mother or father.

Rule number three: ask your accountability partner to put a passcode lock on your smartphone's web browser. This rule forces you to ask for permission to use your web browser. It forces you to explain to another actual human being why you need to get on the internet.

Trust me, I know these rules sound childish. However, when you are addicted to something as serious as lust, you lose some of your rights in the process to recovery. Just like murderers must be locked up in prison, so too should you be restricted so that you can recover and reflect.

No measure is too great in pursuit of strengthening your relationship with Christ. (Of course, so long as it is a biblical measure.) Think about what Jesus said in Mark 9:47, "If your eye causes you to stumble, throw it out; it is better for you to enter the kingdom of God with one eye, than, having two eyes, to be cast into hell" (NASB). In modern terms, if your smartphone causes you to stumble, throw it out; it is better for you to enter the kingdom of God without a phone, than, having an iPhone 20, to be cast into Hell. Sacrificing the little things that cause you to stumble is a small price to pay when you think about the eternal rewards.

Now, it's important to note that this verse is not saying that your actions can save you. It's not the case that you can get rid of the things that cause you to stumble, and then, suddenly, you deserve eternal life. That is nonsense and contrary to the gospel. However, a heart after God that is truly saved will be willing to sacrifice its idols. Moreover, it will *want* to.

As my wise uncle Neill always says, "If Christ is not Lord *of* all, He is not Lord *at* all." If God is not Lord of your smartphone, then He is not Lord of you. If God is not Lord of your laptop, then God is not your Lord. You see, if you are placing your devices (and what you do on them) above God, then God is ranked below those things in your heart. Which, by the very definition of the word, those things have become idols. That is why it is worth literally throwing away your brand new smartphone if it helps you to place Christ as Lord of all. We are really only putting Christ where He rightfully belongs anyway.

Scripture

So let me switch gears. Reading the Bible is sort of like driving. Have you ever driven down a road that you haven't been down in a really long time? Perhaps it is a road you used to drive down every day when you were young, let's say to your high school. If it has been four years since you went down that road, when you finally drive down it again there is a certain feeling you get. It's a feeling of nostalgia, familiarity, and reality. The things that you see give you a feeling of nostalgia, or wistfulness. We long, in some respects, to relive the times of our past. We also get a feeling of familiarity, of course, because we are familiar with the landscape; however, we usually notice things that we didn't notice before, even though we used to drive down this road every day. Also, we get a feeling of reality, or truth, in that what we see is real, tangible, and has a place in our big world.

Similarly, when a Christian reads the very Word of God, he gets a feeling of nostalgia. Not because he has read the words before in his lifetime, but because the Holy Spirit inside of himself knows the words already. So, when the Christian reads them, even for the first time biologically, his spirit recognizes them as familiar because God's Holy Spirit has already known them for an eternity. And we also have a feeling of reality, or truth, in that these words do matter today as much as they did when they were written down. That these words do have a place and an application in the world abroad.

And when it comes to our addictions, the words that we read in the Bible matter with respect to our recovery. The words in the Bible have power. So much so that God Himself, in the form of Jesus, used the Word to battle the temptations of the Devil when He was in the wilderness.

Jesus had fasted forty days and nights at this point, so you can imagine how hungry his flesh must have been. Then, in

Mathew 4:3-4:

> And the tempter came and said to Him, "If You are the Son of God, command that these stones become bread." But [Jesus] answered and said, "It is written, 'Man shall not live on bread alone, but on every word that proceeds out of the mouth of God.'" (NASB)

If you had not eaten food in forty days, can you imagine how tempting it would be to turn those stones to bread and eat? He easily had the power to do this, but He chose to quote scripture as a means to keep from falling into this temptation.

The Devil then tempts Jesus two more times, and Jesus again quotes scripture as a means to battle the temptations. We should follow this example when we are trying to resist temptation, or overcome an addiction. Whenever we are tempted to fall into lust, we should have a few scriptures that we can quote in our minds, or verbally, to help us defeat the Devil.

One scripture that I think we should all memorize is 2nd Timothy 2:22, "So flee youthful passions and pursue righteousness" (ESV). Whenever we are tempted we should immediately quote this scripture, out loud if necessary. This reminds us that we should flee (or run from) whatever is before us that is tempting us. Whether that temptation is coming through an electronic device, or a person, it doesn't matter. We must run from whatever situation is going to cause us to stumble. Furthermore, we should pursue righteousness. We should seek a situation where we can perhaps get into the Word or prayer. These two factors: running *from* lust, and running *to* righteousness, are vital maneuvers to recovery. This one verse is also easy to memorize, so there is no excuse not to have this memorized by the time you put this book down today.

Another verse we should memorize to battle lust is Job 31:1, "I made a covenant with my eyes not to look lustfully at a young woman" (NIV). We should make a covenant, or a promise, to our eyes that we will not look at women lustfully. For instance, whenever we do notice an attractive woman, we should quote this verse as a motivator not to dwell on our sinful thoughts or fantasies. This verse is powerful because it necessitates forethought about what we should do if a situation presents itself in the future. We must already have a game plan before we ever notice a beautiful woman, before we are ever in a tempting situation, rather than waiting until we are in those moments. If we wait until an attractive woman walks by to take control of our mind, it is too late. If we wait until we are alone with our girlfriend on a weekend then it is too late. We must prepare beforehand: spiritually through making a covenant with our eyes, mentally through memorization of scripture, and physically through setting boundaries so that we will be ready when a situation presents itself.

Five Flaming Arrows

FLAMING ARROW #2

WHY DO BAD THINGS

HAPPEN?

Daniel Faucett

LAST TIME ON THE HARDWOOD

Do you ever look back on your life and wish that you could change something? Maybe you would not have asked that girl to prom if you knew she was going to say no. Maybe you would not have eaten chili before your first date. Or maybe you would have studied a little harder for that standardized assessment—you know, the one that determined the college you were going to attend. Whatever the case may be, everyone has something in their past that they wish they could erase, or at least go back and change. You would have to be crazy to reflect on your life and think that you did everything perfectly. For me, the biggest things I regret when I look back on my life are the poor decisions I made, and with each choice, the things I didn't know I was losing.

My best friend, Reed Chambers, once told me about a concept called the "last time," and it goes like this: There is a last time for everything, so make every moment count—you never know, it might be your last time doing that certain thing, or hanging out with that particular person. It's essentially the opposite of "first times." There are many examples of this, such as the last time a father holds his daughter in his arms. At some point, when his daughter gets old enough, he will put her down and never pick her up again. There is going to be the last time you talk to your father, or your mother. It sounds sad, and it is, but it's how our world works. When I look back on my last times, I can't help but think about the last time I played high school basketball.

It was finally my senior year. I had rode the bench mostly as a junior classman, so now it was my time to shine. I had spent the entire off-season playing pick-up basketball every day. I trained harder on my shot than anyone I knew, including some of the other young prospects in the county. I lived, breathed, and drank basketball. It possessed me. (Looking back, I'm surprised I didn't become a basketball.) So, when it came time for our first game, I was beyond ready. I felt like David in the Old Testament, I had my stones close by my side. For me, my stones were represented by hours of preparation spent on my jump shot and three-pointer. The biggest stone in my satchel was represented by my ball handling. I had it all—or at least I did in my head.

The first game of the season was at Weaver High School. The gym was packed, and I had many family, friends, and a pretty girl I was talking to eagerly waiting to see me play. The moment I walked out on that court I knew I was going to have a great night. The old saying was right, with practice comes confidence. The hours I spent practicing revealed themselves that night. I scored 21 points, had 12 assists, and went 9 for 10 from the free-throw line. I was confident, competitive, and a little too proud. While we did lose the game, I was still happy with the way I played.

I guess there is something about playing the game you love in front of the people you love. It is immensely satisfying. Seeing their faces of approval after a win. Even seeing their faces of compassion and sorrow after a loss. Both are sweet. To me, at least at the time, life didn't get better than playing basketball in front of the ones I loved, especially when the gym was packed full.

The hard work that I had put into basketball showed, and it showed to scouts, coaches, teammates and loved ones. I couldn't have been happier with my season opener, the game that I thought would have led me down a season of success, record breaking, and hopefully a college athletic scholarship.

My hopes were high for the sport I loved, but God had different plans for me.

Our second game was at Hokes Bluff High School, where I would be facing against the future Purdue Boilermakers' center, Isaac Haas. Isaac was always tall for his age growing up. I can remember playing with him at the Jacksonville Community Center's PARD league. Back then he was only around six foot, but for a kid in elementary school that was gigantic. By our senior year, Isaac was around seven feet tall. "This game was truly going to be a David and Goliath story," I thought to myself.

Before we went to the game I had received word from my coach that Gadsden State Community College would be pleased to have me join them at their tryouts in the post season. This boosted my confidence, and ego, even more than the successful season opener. My middle school basketball dreams were finally coming true. I was playing my best, and I was being rewarded in exactly the way I wanted to be. Nonetheless, we went to Hokes Bluff and we played against the hero of our little Alabama corner, Isaac Haas.

We had lost our first game, and early into the first quarter it looked like we'd be losing this game also. I had scrapped for 8 points early into the second quarter, but I wasn't happy about the way we were playing. I was mad, and I let my emotions get the best of me for one important play—and that's all it took.

We had a turnover at half court in an attempt to break the press. My teammate, Lucas Ford, and I hustled back to keep the other team from getting a wide-open layup. I bodied up the defender at the right-side block. He shot faked—I didn't bite—then he went up for the shot. I jumped as high as my human body would allow.

At this point in the story I think I should make a confession. My dad warned me at the end of the first quarter to play back and not to foul anymore, but I didn't listen to him. So I swung blindly at the basketball as it was released. I barely skimmed the ball, but I fouled him aggressively.

All of my weight came down on the inside of my right foot. My arms came forward as I prepared for the landing. Another player landed on my back and it forced both of our bodies' weight down on my right foot. The pressure was too much for me. My right ankle broke straight across in a straight line, a clean break across the tibia and fibula.

I rolled over on my back. I slowly lifted my ankle into the air with both hands. I was stunned by what was left of my foot. It looked gruesome, and judging by the silence from the crowd, they thought so too. It was hanging off the end of my leg by a thread. Literally, it was hanging on by what was left of my tendons and skin. There was no bone support for my foot. The displacement was so bad that I would be losing circulation soon in my foot if I did not get to an emergency room for immediate realignment and surgery. (I was told later by a doctor that if I would've been too far from a hospital, perhaps on a mountain somewhere snowboarding, that they might of been forced to amputate my foot.)

You could've heard a pin drop in that gym. Coaches and parents rushed around me, elevating my mangled foot, and speaking words of encouragement to me. I think it was so silent in that gym for two reasons: (a) it was a disgusting injury, and (b) they knew what basketball meant to me. I think their hearts broke for me—or, at least, I would like to believe that they did.

It was one of the saddest moments of my life, and it was the last time that I played basketball in a legitimately sanctioned competition.

As I was wheeled out of the gym on a stretcher, everyone was staring. Completely silent. I didn't wave, and I didn't smile. I was absolutely crushed. It was my last time playing the sport I loved in front of the people I loved, so I didn't feel like smiling. One realignment, nine screws and a metal plate later, I was back into rehab. Still practicing my dribbling in the hopes that I would return to the game that I loved.

It ended up taking another surgery and two years of rehabilitation to get back to where I was, but of course it was too late for me. I had missed the Gadsden State tryouts, and any other tryouts that may have come after a full season. I was now just another guy who hooped in the college recreation center—who also had a killer X-ray to show off.

FIGURE 6.1

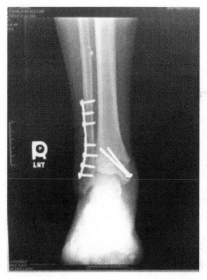

The good news is that during my recovery time after my first surgery, I studied religiously for the ACT. When it came time for the exam, I crutched into the testing center with a highly protective boot—probably a little high on painkillers—and made a thirty. I then applied for the Elite Scholarship at Jacksonville State University and received it. It included housing, a meal plan, and full tuition. A total value of over sixty thousand dollars.

However, I do not take credit for my ACT score, I give all the glory, honor, and credit to God; because I believe He blessed me with the conditions to succeed on that exam. God gave me a healthy mind and three months locked in a bed with an ACT prep book. Most people are not fortunate enough to have such conditions to prepare for the ACT. Even my teachers had made arrangements to help me succeed. My history teacher, Mr. Findley, provided me with an ACT prep book to study while I was recovering. My physics teacher, Mr. Jackson, helped me by streamlining the remainder of his course and providing me with handwritten notes on the course. My literature teacher, Mrs. Roe, also streamlined her course to make it more manageable while I was away from school. God worked in so many ways to help me succeed. I guess for some odd reason He wanted me to have that scholarship.

Not everyone gets the opportunity to be alone for three months, and to be able to study for one exam. Most seniors in high school have a million things to worry about, I had one thing, and it was to make a great score on the ACT.

Also, during my recovery, I bonded with the greatest woman I have ever met, Bailey Underwood. She came to my house almost every day to bring me food and to keep me company. She helped keep my spirits up in a dark time. It was through my recovery that Bailey and I truly fell in love. While it was nearly a year after that ankle-shattering night that I told her I loved her, I knew I did back then. She was the girl of my dreams. She loved God, she valued the Bible, and she clearly cared for me more than any other person I knew.

In addition to falling for my future wife, I also reevaluated what it was that I treasured in life. Was it basketball that I valued as number one? Or was it Jesus Christ? Why was I able to put so much time and effort into a sport, but I wasn't willing to give the Creator of everything ten minutes of prayer? I had been valuing a sport over my Savior. But during this time of recovery, my relationship with God, through Christ, began to grow deeper as I finally spent time with Him. It took something as drastic as this injury for me to finally sit still, and simply recognize that God wanted my heart.

If I had not received that scholarship to JSU, then I probably would have continued my education at Gadsden State Community College. I would have gotten my basics there, then I would have transferred to JSU to major in exercise science, and I would have applied to PT school. I would've become a physical therapist as I pursued money and comfort. However, since I went to JSU, I decided to major in General Science and Education because I felt that I could have a bigger impact. After all, I had reevaluated what it was that I valued in life, and Christ was number one now. So, I decided that becoming a teacher, and serving my students every day for the rest of my life, would be the best way to show Christ's love, and to change this next generation for the better.

But let's get back to the concept of "last times." This ankle break represents the last time that I played basketball in a legitimately sanctioned competition. So, the question I have to ask myself is this: If I could go back in time, would I change what happened that night in Hokes Bluff's gym?

I wouldn't change a thing.

If it were not for me breaking my ankle that night, I never would have made a thirty on my ACT. I never would have majored in General Science and Education. I never would have fallen in love with my future wife, Bailey. And most importantly, I never would have reevaluated and reestablished my relationship with God. God got my attention back then, and I'm glad He did.

While this is an example of a last time that I wouldn't change, I have one more last time to share with you that is an example of the other. An example of something that I desperately would change if I had the chance to.

7

LAST TIME WITH STEVEN HUDDLESTON

Everyone in my family of seven were homeschooled through the sixth grade by my mom. Every time someone in our family got into the seventh grade, they went to public school so they could play sports at a more competitive level. When I was in the sixth grade, my older brothers, Joseph and David, played on the varsity football team at Pleasant Valley High School. I would often go to their football games on Friday nights with my parents to watch them play. It was there that I met Steven Huddleston.

He was with some of his buddies throwing football behind the stands on this small grassy hill. (If you are a member of the

Pleasant Valley community, you know exactly what hill I am referring to.) This hill is the hangout for all of the elementary kids who go to the varsity football games. When I arrived, I noticed Steven was wearing a Pleasant Valley Elementary football jersey. He was clearly the leader of the group of kids. In my homeschooled and awkward way, I walked up to them and tried to play. After all, the homeschoolers that I knew were very welcoming; so I assumed these kids would be too. While some were because they discovered I was a member of the athletically renowned Faucett family, Steven was not very impressed.

I'm not really sure what started the fight, but somehow Steven and I got into a brawl. I tackled him, he pushed me, and we wrestled on the grass for a few minutes until someone broke us up. From that point on, I didn't exactly have a good opinion of the guy. I mean who tries to fight someone the first time they meet them? Nevertheless, kids have an odd social system, so back then it probably made perfect sense why we were fighting.

After the fight cooled down, I went back to sit with my parents. At the end of the game I left without seeing Steven again. To be precise, I didn't see him again until a varsity basketball game later that year.

My friend Dalton Bean was filming the game, so I sat with him when I arrived at the gym. At this point, the fight with

Steven wasn't really on my mind anymore; that is, until Steven walked in the door across the gym floor. He was wearing an NFL jersey and jeans as he walked across the gym with his head down. He was bobbing his slouched head and chewing gum as if he was listening to music. I saw him approaching the stands looking for someone. I assumed he wouldn't sit with Dalton and me.

He saw us, and my heart started racing. *This kid isn't going to come up here and try to fight again, is he?* Sure enough, Steven moseyed up the stairs and sat right between Dalton and me. It was silent for about three seconds. Then, Steven turned to me and reached out his hand to shake mine. I obliged, but I was shocked when I noticed his hands were abnormally large. *This was a kid, but his hands were like an NBA player's,* I thought to myself. Later he demonstrated his amazing ability to palm a full-size basketball, but that's beside the point. We were "cool" now, and from that point on our friendship blossomed.

It was the only friendship I've ever made that started with a physical fight. I guess it was something about that fight that earned his respect, and that earned mine also. What truly earned my respect from Steven wasn't necessarily that he fought me, but that he was willing to extend his hand as a friend *after* he fought me. Not only did he extend his hand of friendship, but he extended it first. I knew there was something special about a guy who was willing to swallow his pride, and admit that something he did was wrong. We even talked about the fight that night and had a good laugh about it. Ironically, it was that fight that became a fun explanation of our friendship. It represented the cornerstone of forgiveness that made our relationship something unique.

Once Steven got into high school—which at Pleasant Valley included 7th through 12th grades—we started to hangout regularly. We would often find ourselves playing basketball until 1:00 AM in the morning in his driveway. (We played all our games with this fuzzy basketball that was extremely old. It was fuzzy because it had been played with so much that the vinyl covering was peeling off, but the remains were still held on by the adhesive residues; hence, it had strings of fuzz extending out all around it like a shag carpet.) We also rode our bikes all over the PV community, Piedmont, and the city of Jacksonville. We ate a lot of Smiley's—which were a fruity gummy snack that we were addicted to. What was most memorable, though, was when we talked about girls, our family, and God.

Throughout high school we would periodically hangout, but much less often than we did in middle school. When we did, however, it was like we picked up right where we left off. We would talk about girls, God, and our families in more depth, and from much more spiritual perspectives. Now that we were older, it seemed like we knew it all when it came to our faith. We talked about predestination, salvation, and how to live a life that reflected Christ. In hindsight, I am so thankful that we had those conversations about God, but more on that later.

The last time I saw Steven Huddleston was also at a football game at Pleasant Valley High School—just like the first time that we met. We talked during the game and caught up about our lives. He was going through some program at Gadsden State Community College, and I was continuing my studies at Jacksonville State University.

Before I left that evening, Steven asked me if I wanted to hangout soon. I, with my "busy" freshman schedule, regretfully declined. This was one of the biggest mistakes of my life. You see, I tend to make myself a schedule, and I stick to it like it's the Bible. If anything, or anyone gets in the way of my schedule, then I don't hang out with that person or do that particular thing. If I would have known that that would have been the last time that I saw Steven, you better believe I would have hung out with him. I would've skipped class in a heartbeat. Heck, I would have dropped out of school.

You can't put a price on the life of a friend, or the time you get to spend with them. No sacrifice of mine would have compared to being able to see him again. It was not long after that night, on November 4th, 2014, that Steven Huddleston died in a car accident. Here is an excerpt from the Anniston

Star about his accident:

> A 17-year-old driver died in a single-vehicle crash north of Jacksonville on Tuesday. Kevin Cook, a public information officer for the Alabama State Troopers, said Huddleston was driving a 2005 Honda Accord when the car left the roadway and overturned at around 11:15 p.m. According to Cook, Huddleston was not wearing a seatbelt and was thrown from the vehicle.[1]

I got the call the next morning. I could hear Bailey's voice on the other end shaking as she told me the horrible news. I kept asking her, "Is it true?" As she cried, I knew her heart was breaking for me. Personally, I was in disbelief. I was in shock. I just laid there and cried. It was my first taste of death, or at least death that hit my heart so personally. I had seen death from older family members and acquaintances, but not until Steven died did I experience the death of someone I was friends with—someone I was really close to. The sting of sin and death hit my heart at its core that day.

My last time seeing Steven was spent talking at a football game as great friends, while my first time seeing Steven was spent having a brawl. I like the contrast of those two nights. However, while we had great conversations that last night, they were unfortunately short lived. I wish I could've had more time with him.

I think it's important to note that there is a huge difference in my last time playing basketball and my last time spent with Steven Huddleston. My last time on the hardwood I left it all on the court. I had no regrets. Twelve years of blood sweat and tears I poured into that sport, and I believe God had a purpose for everything that happened through my ankle break. Through that experience, God brought me closer into His arms, steered me into a different career direction, and taught me where He should rank in my heart. Through that experience, I am now able to relate to others who missed out on the sport they loved (such as my younger brother, Joshua, who had a similar injury that ruined his senior year), or who simply had a catastrophic event that changed their life. However, with Steven Huddleston, the experience was different.

But before we discuss the bad, let's focus on the good.

The death of Steven Huddleston was a wakeup call for everyone who knew him. A call to reevaluate our faith in Christ. When I heard the news of his death, I fearfully considered his eternal destination, and what he was experiencing. Thankfully, I was able to remember the conversations that we had together about our faith in Christ. They may have been from the perspectives of "baby Christians," but they were on the foundation that is Jesus, and that gives me comfort. If the basis of our faith was on anything else, such as by works, then I would be fearful of where Steven ended up. I would be unsure, but since I know what we based our faith on (that is Christ), I can rest assured that Steven is with Him now in heaven. Because the promises of Christ—salvation, eternity, redemption, grace, mercy, forgiveness, and a relationship—are trustworthy.

Besides being a wake-up call to reevaluate our faith in Christ, it was also a warning proclaiming to all that we do not have an eternity on this Earth. Whether you die at seventeen, like Steven, or seventy you still must face death. According to Psalm 144:4, "Man is like a breath; his days are like a passing shadow." (ESV). You may find this comparison to be untrue, that our life is as brief as a breath. However, in comparison to eternity, this is very true. Our life is like a grain of sand dropped in the ocean, when the entire ocean is considered, the sand grain becomes relatively tiny. When eternity is considered, our life and its timeline becomes tinier than a grain of sand.

The death of Steven Huddleston led Zade Adams and me to consider ways in which we could honor his life. We decided that the best way to do that would be to share Steven's testimony and to incorporate, somehow, the game of basketball. We figured that a basketball camp would be the perfect way to accomplish those two goals. So, Zade Adams and I set up a camp with the help of Brad Hood.

We did a lot of research on effective basketball drills, and we worked with Steven's parents, Wanda and Duane, through the whole process. The Steven Huddleston Basketball Camp symbol (see Figure 7.1) was actually designed from a picture I took of Steven dunking one afternoon at Pam Scott's house (which was a safe and supervised place for teenagers to hang out in the PV community).

Since starting, we have had the Steven Huddleston Basketball Camp for three consecutive years. Each year it has been an amazing experience of basketball and gospel-centered talks. This past summer (2017) we had our biggest turnout in the camp's history. Nineteen kids from kindergarten through the sixth grade came, and many adults and high school ball players came and contributed to the camp. For 2018, we have even bigger plans to expand the camp to multiple locations.

FIGURE 7.1

In 2017, donations poured in as the Lord blessed our camp through First Church in Rainbow City, Alabama. In combination with the Huddleston family and pastor Jeff Underwood's church, each kid who attended received a free t-shirt and a free basketball. The basketballs were later signed by a college basketball player friend of mine, Jon Stone, who came to the camp and showed off his dunks for the kids.

It was beautiful to see so many kids playing the sport that Steven and I bonded through. The sport that we both loved. To see these kids hear the message that resonates from Steven's life. Among these messages were "Don't wait to get right with God. Your life is short. The days are evil. Make the most of the time you have with your family and friends." These messages needed to be taught, and along with teaching the fundamentals of basketball, it became a very fun, heartwarming, and memorable experience for the community.

Just like I always say at Hudd Camp, my encouragement to you is to cherish every moment you have with the people you love. Cherish every moment you have with the things you love to do. And most importantly, don't wait to get right with the Lord. If I knew that night at Pleasant Valley was going to be my last night spent with Steven Huddleston, I would have shut out the noise of my life. I would have stayed up all night spending time with him. I would have hung out with him the following week when he wanted to hang out with me. I would have skipped class and taken a B on an assignment for once in my life—an insignificant sacrifice to be able to see someone for the last time.

It's a simple point: You never know when it's going to be the last time you will see someone. At some point in your life, it will be the last time you see your wife, your mom, and maybe even your own child. So I think this whole experience sheds light on how we should treat others. We should treat them like they are ephemeral, because they are all passing from this life to the next very quickly. The only thing that matters is the lives that we impact for the next life.

Additionally, through this experience of losing Steven, I am reminded of Romans 10:11, "WHOEVER BELIEVES IN HIM WILL NOT BE DISAPPOINTED" (NASB). I guarantee you that Steven is not disappointed. If you could ask Steven today what He thinks about our Savior—now that he has seen Him face-to-face—I guarantee you his passion and appreciation would put any praise our Lord has received on this Earth to shame.

Five Flaming Arrows

WHY DO BAD THINGS HAPPEN?

While there are many good things that came from Steven's death, I still have trouble understanding why bad things like this happen. The death of Steven felt dark. It felt deeply spiritual. Almost as if somewhere in the spiritual realm Satan had defeated Steven's guardian angel in a battle. Once this occurred, he was able to steer that vehicle off the road. But why? Why would God allow Satan to take the life of Steven? If God is all-powerful, why does He allow anything bad to happen?

The simple answer is sin. The complicated answer is God's infinite sovereignty. And the secular answer is bad things happen simply because they do. All answers I have reservations with when they are taken as the only possible explanation. First, let's establish that sin is the cause of bad things. To do this, we must revisit the Garden of Eden.

The Garden of Eden

Satan, in the form of a serpent, comes to Eve in the Garden of Eden near the tree of knowledge of good and evil. (It is important to note, before continuing, that God had previously warned Adam and Eve that if they ate from this tree that they would die.) Satan, in his deceptive nature, comes to Eve in Genesis 3:3 and says, "You will not certainly die . . . For God knows that when you eat from it your eyes will be opened, and you will be like God, knowing good and evil" (NIV). Take note that Satan tells her a lie coupled cleverly with a truth, in order to make his words more tempting. The truth is that they would become more like God, knowing good and evil—which is later established as truth in verse twenty-two. However, Satan lies when he says that Eve will not certainly die. Later, Adam, Eve, and all of humanity are cursed with the existence of death as punishment. Therefore, Satan used the mingling of a truth with a lie in order to more effectively tempt Eve. In today's world, we see this same satanic method being used all of the time. Nevertheless, continuing in Genesis chapter three and verse six:

When the woman saw that the fruit of the tree was good for food and pleasing to the eye, and also desirable for gaining wisdom, she took some and ate it. She also gave some to her husband, who was with her, and he ate it. Then the eyes of both of them were opened, and they realized they were naked; so they sewed fig leaves together and made coverings for themselves. (NIV)

Adam and Eve did not sin by finding the tree's fruit desirable. They couldn't help but recognize the beauty of it. Therefore, being tempted is not a sin, we cannot avoid temptations because they are all around us. Even Jesus Christ was tempted. Additionally, temptation clearly existed through Satan's words *before* Adam and Eve ever brought sin to humanity, and Adam and Eve were not punished for being tempted. However, falling and submitting to temptation is sin, and that's where Adam and Eve fell short. When they took and ate the fruit, they deliberately disobeyed a perfect and holy God. And as you know, disobeying God has penalties.

A penalty is defined as a punishment imposed for breaking a law, rule, or contract.[2] In the Garden of Eden, Adam and Eve had been given a rule (or a law) not to eat of a certain tree, but they did anyway. Therefore, they brought judgement on themselves, and we now have inherited a punishment—or penalty—for what they did. What does this punishment entail? According to Genesis chapter three: separation from God, the existence of death, and the presence of pain.

In the Garden, Adam and Eve had a relationship with God that was uninhibited by sin because sin was not yet in them. While direct and physical "walking-with-God" interaction has been debated by writers such as Tim Chaffey, the text reveals that Adam and Eve had an intimate relationship with God—whether more spiritually than face-to-face is not necessarily that important to the central message of our history. Either way, God had a personal relationship with Adam and Eve before they took and ate of the fruit, and that relationship was uninhibited by sin. This means that there was no barrier between God and man that now exists because of sin.

When they took and ate of the fruit, part of our punishment was a separation and polarization. In Genesis 3:22-24, God sends Adam and Eve out of the Garden after they had sinned. This represents the newfound separation between God and man. A new reality we can call the sin barrier. Isaiah the prophet in Isaiah 59:2 reiterates the reality of the sin barrier, "But your iniquities have made a separation between you and your God, And your sins have hidden *His* face from you so that He does not hear" (NASB).

We are not only separated *from* God, but we are polarized *to* God. In science, "Polarity is defined as having two opposite tendencies or opposite electrical charges."[3] God and man now have opposite charges, and we definitely have opposite tendencies. Man tends to want what his sinful flesh craves: gluttony, idolatry, pornography, selfishness, etc. God wants for man what His Spirit gives: love, joy, peace, patience, kindness, goodness, faithfulness, gentleness, and self-control. With these two opposite charges, or tendencies, in place, there is a natural polarization between God and man. We naturally crave the opposite of God. Galatians 5:17 tells us, "For the flesh sets its desire against the Spirit, and the Spirit against the flesh; for these are in opposition to one another, so that you may not do the things that you please" (NASB).

But back to the original question: Why do bad things happen? They happen because of our separation from God and our polarization to God. Simply put, our sin has had intense consequences—that is, that *we* can't help but do bad things. That is why we need God's divine intervention. Because without Him we are lost in our own way, and in our own sin. And in our depraved state we do extremely evil things. So without Him living in us, we will always have the opposite charge of God and the tendency of sin. This charge and tendency causes *us* to do really bad things.

So if you want God to stop bad things from happening, then where do you want Him to start? Truly, if He is going to stop bad things from happening, then He better take every person on this Earth off of it—*we* are the problem. As long as we are here, and as long as we have the free will to choose sin, bad things are going to happen.

But can we pursue self-righteousness in the hopes of abolishing evil?

Sin is Like Gravity

I think it helps our understanding of sin if we can imagine that it is like gravity. It's constantly pulling us down. Never wavering. No matter how far we are away from the surface of the Earth, gravity will always be pulling down on us. Mainly because the force of gravity exerted on us is determined by our mass, the mass of Earth, and the distance between these two objects' geometric centers. Therefore, no matter how far away we are from Earth, there will always be a distance between us and the Earth. There will always be the Earth, and there will always be us. Therefore, this force will only gradually decrease in magnitude, but will never completely go away. You cannot separate yourself from this force. Likewise, with sin, no matter how much good you do, on your own you cannot separate yourself from the force of it. No matter if you live a near perfect life, without Jesus Christ's gift of salvation, you will still be pulled down to Hell because of the force of sin. You will still commit terrible atrocities. If you have not allowed Christ to be Lord of all, then *you* will be your own lord, and that is a very dangerous condition. Sin is a strong force, and it has you from the day that you are born. I think it is obvious that only

Christ can overcome it.

If this was a book—which technically it is—I guess I just ruined the point to the whole thing: that is, that Jesus is the solution to our spiritual problem of sin. So if there's anything to learn from Steven's death—which his life was much more than lessons to be learned—it is that we do not have infinite time on this Earth.

So bad things happen because of our sin, but what about death in general? According to Romans 6:23, "For the wages of sin is death." (ESV). It's simply the consequence, or byproduct, of our sin. Literally billions of people around the globe have died, and continue to die, because of Adam and Eve's sin (see Romans 5:12). Every second, nearly two people die. Every minute, 105. Every hour, 6,316. Every day, 151,600. Every year, 55.3 million.[4] According to these statistics, death is as prevalent as breathing. So, how can we be free from death and sin?

In Ephesians 6:16, the Word tells us that we should take up our shield of faith, so that we can extinguish the flaming arrows of the Evil One. Therefore, Death and sin are spiritual arrows that the Devil launches at us. He uses them to destroy us. We must exercise our faith in Christ to overcome them. So, if we are without Christ, what can we do? Truthfully, we will be destroyed.

Without my faith in Christ, I would not be able to

overcome the weight of death that bears down on me in situations like Steven's. Through Christ, Steven Huddleston was saved, and is now with Him in heaven. Through Christ, according to 2nd Timothy 2:10, we too can experience "the salvation that is in Christ Jesus with eternal glory" (ESV).

Last summer I was giving a Bible lesson at the end of the 2017 Steven Huddleston Basketball Camp. There were many parents and students who were there sitting on the gym floor that hot summer afternoon, waiting to be fed with the Word of God. It felt good to take a moment and share with them the good news of Jesus Christ. But it was bitter sweet because, at the same time, I had to share the reality of death. To truly share Steven's story we must talk about it. So, we looked to First Corinthians 15:50-57.

According to these verses, the sting of death is sin, and we cannot separate ourselves from sin completely while we are on this Earth. People often say that our victory over death is in Christ, and that is true; however, until Christ comes back again, at the last trumpet, sin and the *sting* of death will still exist. We will still suffer their effects because sin and physical death have not yet been destroyed.

There is a separation between my friend Steven and me because of sin. Until the last trumpet sounds, and sin and death are no more, there will be a pain felt over the loss of loved ones, even the ones who have died with Christ in their heart.

While knowing that Steven had Jesus in his heart softens the sting, the sting and pain is still felt because of our separation. First Corinthians 15:25-26, "For he must reign until he has put all his enemies under his feet. The last enemy to be destroyed is death" (ESV). Death comes down last of all, and I can't wait for that day.

However, even if we have a biblical understanding that the wages of sin is death, and that we can be saved from death and eternal Hell through Christ, it can still be difficult to wrap our minds around the gravity of sin. It seems like such an extreme penalty, *if God is so loving, why would He allow so many people to die?* Not only the people who die, but *what about those who die without Christ? Are they supposed to go to Hell simply because of Adam and Eve?*

When you take scripture out of context, it sounds crazy and unsupported for death, punishment, suffering, judgement, and eternal separation from God to even exist. However, when you look to the entire Word for a more full picture of the character of God, then you can begin to understand why the penalty for sin is so severe.

All of God's character qualities must be exhibited in some capacity; otherwise, scripture would be lying to us about who God is. For example, the Bible talks about God's wrath, but if there was never any exhibited wrath from God, then scripture would be lying to us about Him. Therefore, it makes sense that all of God's character qualities are exhibited.

God's wrath and justice are exhibited in eternal judgement of unbelievers, and the punishment of sin. God's love is exhibited in His Son, Jesus Christ, and by those who come to know Him. God's peace is exhibited through His Holy Spirit, especially when He guards our hearts and our minds from anxiety. God's joy is seen in the rejoicing of believers— especially the supernatural rejoicing of Christians amidst trials and tribulations.

Therefore, for all of God's character qualities to be true (which this is not a comprehensive list), there must be an exhibition of each that can be seen in some capacity. This is why God is a God of love *and* wrath. A God of joy *and* justice. He is a God who doesn't lie to us about who He is. While we may not like the idea of Hell, at least we can appreciate God's honesty with us through His Word. His consistency of truth, His warning of the wrath to come, and His offering of love through His Son. So I guess my point is this: at least He doesn't lie to us.

What people want, however, is a God of love, but not a God of wrath. A God of joy, but not a God of ultimate justice. People want to pick and choose the character qualities of God that they want, rather than looking at the Word objectively to get to know God for who He is.

I think this is why we see other religions and cults sprout

up all around the world. People like to mold themselves around a god that *they* like, not the One that actually exists. Because the One that truly exists has some things to say about the way we live our lives.

God tells us about ourselves spiritually through the Bible. Just like that friend who tells us physical things about ourselves that we don't want to hear. For example, my brother Nathan is extremely blunt and straightforward. If you look like you've gained a few pounds, he'll tell you. He really doesn't care if it hurts your feelings, he just makes it known that you've gained some weight, and that you probably should start exercising. Not necessarily in a mean way, but just honestly tells you what he thinks. And I think at some level we need people like that in our lives. My friend Patton Chambers is exactly the same way, and that's probably why he and Nathan are such good friends.

But in truth, you appreciate the friends who tell you the truth rather than telling you what you want to hear. People pleasers are quick to make you feel good about yourself, but they aren't helping you any by lying to your face. We need people to tell us the truth so we can have an honest assessment of ourselves. So we can improve and adapt. Perhaps it's better sometimes to have that truth seasoned and softened on the corners a little bit before being presented to us, but it is still needed. Likewise, the Bible tells us spiritual truth about Hell and suffering, and people don't want to hear it. Just like people don't want to listen to their straightforward friends.

No one wants to be told that they are sinful and of an inherently depraved mind. Not only that, but that they cannot make themselves holy on their own. We are born into sin and therefore deserve condemnation. And most importantly, we are unable to save ourselves. It may not be what you *want* to hear, but it definitely is what you *need* to hear.

9

GOD'S SOVEREIGNTY

Sin is an explanation of why bad things happen. However, there are other reasons why bad things happen. One such reason is God's infinite sovereignty. Sovereignty is defined as supreme excellence and power; freedom from external control, as well as being a controlling influence.[5] To put it simply, the word *control* is a synonym for sovereignty. By using this definition of sovereignty, then we can conclude that God is in control of everything; which means He is in control even during terrible situations.

A long time ago I went to my uncle Neill's house in Dallas, Georgia with my whole family on a Saturday night. The next morning, we decided to go to my uncle's church down the street where he would be teaching Sunday school. My entire family attended this Sunday school class. It was geared for kids around the 5th grade, but the lesson packed a spiritual punch that would have made the likes of John Piper proud.

I can't remember all the Bible verses that accompanied the lesson, but I know that my uncle shared an example of God's sovereignty that I'll never forget. He gave a hypothetical situation. He said, "Suppose someone pulls a gun on you and shoots you." He made the appropriate hand motions as he chose a kid for an example. "Ok, so could God have stopped this from happening?" He waited for the kids' responses. They all basically said *yes* because God can do anything. Which I couldn't disagree with; after all, God is all-powerful and can do anything that is logically possible. My uncle then went on to ask, "Does that mean that God killed you, or that God wanted you to die?"

The room was quiet. It was obvious that this situation just got a lot deeper. We were now thinking about the *motive* of God. Essentially we were questioning if God is good—or at least as good as the Bible makes Him out to be. We were questioning God's motives because if God is sovereign, which He is, then He is in control of situations where people die. He could stop all of the bad things from happening. So, if He doesn't stop bad things from happening, does He *want* them to happen?

The believing families—who have lost loved ones—they know that God is good, but they understand especially that He is all-powerful. They know that God can do whatever He wills. They know that God could have saved their lost loved ones from dying. If God wanted to save Steven Huddleston from flipping his car and dying that night on November 4th, He could have. If God wanted to save the children who are taken advantage of from their suffering, He could. If God wanted to establish world peace and end all suffering at this very moment, He could. Because God is all-powerful and in complete control, and nothing can take place without Him knowing it. Therefore, God could stop suffering and pain.

But God doesn't stop them, they still exist. People are murdered, raped, stolen from, and aborted. When you consider God's sovereignty, it is easy to go down the path of ungratefulness. We think we would be better at being God because at least we wouldn't let people die, right? However, God's will *is* perfect. And when God allows bad things to happen, we must understand that there is a reason for it.

For instance, God created the tree of knowledge of good and evil to be in the Garden of Eden, knowing full well that Adam and Eve would eat the fruit. He knew that they would bring sin into the world, and that He would have to send His one and only Son to die for those sins. We may not like that

He allows us to do bad things, but at least He offers His grace that can redeem us from them.

We may never understand the reasons for all the bad things in the world until we meet God face-to-face; but either way, we must also realize one important truth: God doesn't cause the evil in the world, *we* do. God didn't cause Adam and Eve to eat of the tree, they used their own free will to do so. We use our own free will to kill, commit adultery, and murder babies in the womb. We are the evil in the world, not God. Yes, God allows bad things to happen, and for Satan to get away with terrible things at the moment, but God is not causing these evil things to happen. There is a significant difference.

We may disagree with what He allows to happen, but that doesn't mean that we know better than Him. He is weaving a much bigger picture that we are not cognizant of. Our time frame of life, whether seventeen or eighty years, is much too small to understand all of the reasons why bad things happen.

I imagine that all of time is like a ten-thousand-piece puzzle, and our lifetime is one piece. How are we to know the puzzle's image when we only have one piece to contribute? Of course, we can read scripture, and through that we can understand what this puzzle will look like in the end. Since we were created for God's glory, then in the end, that is exactly what this puzzle's image will represent. However, the technical aspect of where each piece goes, and what each piece will look like, eludes us. I think that is the hardest part: that we do not know how each piece will fit into this puzzle.

God is in Control

Proverbs 19:21 says, "Many are the plans in the mind of a man, but it is the purpose of the Lord that will stand" (ESV). While we may try to plan out every step of our lives, and prevent any harm from coming our way, we really do not have control over anything. It is God's purpose for our lives that will come to fruition. I am personally thankful for this because it takes away worry. Since God is in control, and His purpose for my life will stand, all I can do is try my absolute best to follow His Son's example, and trust that He will provide.

If I got things the way I wanted them all the time, then I never would have broken my ankle, and I never would have learned the lessons that I learned from that situation. Through braking my ankle, I developed character. I learned to deal with suffering. I learned to cope with disappointments. And most importantly, I learned humility. I learned that taking a backseat on the bench so others can shine can be more rewarding than being the star. While I still have leaps and bounds to make in these areas, through that terrible situation, God gave me a lot of spiritual growth.

Romans 8:28 says, "And we know that for those who love God all things work together for good, for those who are called according to his purpose" (ESV). While I already am understanding why I broke my ankle, I do not know if I will ever understand why God allowed Steven to be taken from his family. It is easy to see the spiritual fruit and character that came as a result of me breaking my ankle; however, it is harder to see the reason why God let Steven die. I may never understand it until the day I meet Jesus and Steven again in heaven. But for now, all I can do is cling to Romans 8:28 and hope that our infinitely sovereign Lord has a reason. After all, God's ways are higher than our ways. His thoughts, plans, and purposes are superior to ours. Therefore, who am I to judge the motive of God?

Should a clay cup argue with the potter as to why he made him a cup, and not a bowl? Does not the potter know more about the purpose of his creation than does the created thing? Likewise, we are God's creation, and we have no right to argue with the way God made us, what conditions He gave us from birth, or when we will die. God, our potter and Creator, knows more about the purpose of our condition on Earth, and what fruit will come from it, than we do. We must rest and trust in Him.

We don't understand why bad things are happening in the moment that they do, but we must realize that God sees things from an eternal perspective. He can see everything that is happening, everything that has happened, and everything that will happen for all of eternity. The bad things that happen today may actually have a positive effect on the future. Perhaps the effect of Steven's death in the future will be a revival. We may never see that revival, perhaps the greatest effect of Steven's death, but that doesn't mean God isn't planning one. The time frame we are cognizant of is too small to see all of the reasons why God allows bad things to happen.

Omnipotence and Wisdom

I think Jacques Marie Louis Monsabre, a wise priest of old, described it best when he said the following:

> If God would concede me His omnipotence for twenty-four hours, you would see how many changes I would make in the world. But if He gave me His wisdom too, I would leave things as they are.[6]

We do not possess God's wisdom or His omnipotence; hence, we cannot fully understand why bad things happen. However, I wonder how differently we would see the course of human history if we did possess these powers. Perhaps there is a method to the madness. Perhaps we wouldn't change a thing if we knew His wisdom.

Daniel Faucett

FLAMING ARROW #3

SCIENCE

Daniel Faucett

10

ATHEISTS

It is wrong to assume that all atheists have been hurt by Christians, or that all atheists are... fill in the blank. Truly, all atheists are different and unique and have their own story and reason for believing what they believe—or, more accurately put, what they *don't* believe. Many atheists, including my own brother John, are atheists—at least for now—because they believe the data supports their proposition. The proposition that a creator is improbable or impossible. And that years of study, research, and the application of the scientific method have reasserted that fact. However, I will argue that the data supports the theory of Intelligent Design (ID): that much of matter, complexity, and order can best be explained by an intelligent cause.

But first, we must establish what is at stake. Putting your faith in Christ is hard, if it was easy then everyone would be an authentic and on-fire Christ follower. You have to die to yourself and let God become the ruler of your life. Christ tells us that we will be persecuted as Christians for our faith, and Paul tells us that we can count all our losses for the sake of Christ as gains for the Kingdom. However, to be an atheist is also hard, you are the minority anywhere you go—except perhaps with college professors in biology departments. But in the *real* and regular world, people will argue with you until they are blue in the face to try and change your mind on your atheistic views. Atheists are often outcasts of their families, and even treated poorly because of their views. Therefore, I believe whichever you identify with—Christianity or atheism—you will be persecuted in some capacity.

In many ways, I respect atheists near to the degree I respect sold-out Christians. Because atheists are honest about what they believe, and what they think. They don't care who thinks less of them because of their views, they just have confidence in what they think is true, and they hold on to that stronger than many Christians hold on to the truth of scripture. I think a lot can be learned from the boldness of atheists.

The truth is, however, that there is too much at stake to

consider being an atheist. What if the atheist is wrong? What if God does exist? Then he or she has thrown eternity away; they have trashed and ignored eternal salvation. They will face eternal judgement, and worst of all, separation from God. However, if you're a Christian and you're wrong, then God doesn't exist and it doesn't matter. Because you will end up just like the atheist. You both will go into nothingness, experiencing nothing with no consciousness.

Of course, if there were no evidence for Intelligent Design, then it would not be foolish to consider atheism. The problem, however, as you will see in this section of my book, is that there is overwhelming evidence for ID theory. (And that is the unsettling aspect of living in our universe: there are too many things that point to an intelligent cause.)

Now, there are two types of atheists: those who wouldn't believe in God if He was shown to be true, and those who would. So if you're an atheist, then you must ask yourself this question, "Would I believe in God if He was proven to be true?" If your answer to that question is *no*, then you have a problem of the *will*. It's not the evidence that is a barrier to you, it is your heart. I think it is helpful for the atheist to analyze his own heart at this point before moving forward with this book.

But back to the idea that eternity is at stake. I want you to imagine a balance. On the right side we have the idea that God doesn't exist. On the left side we have the idea that He does. We can start adding the consequences of each one being true if you believe the other viewpoint—represented by weights. So one consequence of adopting atheism would be eternal hell—which would be represented by a weight on the side for God's existence. This scale would be busting through the floor on the left side representing that God does exist because there is so much at stake if this viewpoint is true. The real question, therefore, is not whether God exists, but rather which God to believe in. The God of the Christian Bible, or the God of the Quran? Buddhism or Hinduism? How do I know who is telling the truth?

The truth is the God of the Bible, and to save another 200 pages on the topic, I'll put it simply: The God of the Christian Bible is the only God that doesn't require vain good works in order to achieve a righteous standing with Him. The Bible tells us that God reached down from heaven to us. He did all the work for us, and we have done nothing. He came down and died for us so that we can have a relationship with Him. In Christianity, God did it all, we have nothing to do with earning our salvation, and God wants to have a personal relationship with us.

In other religions, there is no absolute assurance of salvation because there is no way to tell if you have done enough good works to go to Heaven. In Christianity, we know that Christ—the perfect and sinless Son of God who came as a man—was a sufficient sacrifice for the forgiveness of our sins. He was sufficient because He was blameless and perfect. We can rest in Christ, and this gives us a peace that is unmatched. In other words, we have the ultimate assurance of salvation because it rests on what God did for us, not on what we did for Him.

Now concerning one mental barrier for the atheist. The thing that I want all readers to understand about the six-day creation, and molecules-to-man evolution, is that neither of them can be proven. I cannot prove that God exists or made the world, but neither can man prove that molecules-to-man evolution is absolute truth. They are both only ideas that can be supported by our observations; all we can do is look at data, and see which idea the data most closely supports. What is important to note is that you are not unscientific for interpreting data from a biblical perspective, or an evolutionary perspective, those are simply ideologies that influence your thinking and reasoning and the way in which you see the facts.

For example, in the fossil record there are organisms that seem like intermediate organisms—a lifeform that was in an "intermediate" stage of evolutionary development when fossilized. Perhaps the organism looks like a fish, but it has hind legs. So, the data is that we have an organism that looks like a fish with hind legs. There are many interpretations for this data, but the interpretations are *not* facts. The evolutionary interpretation (which is not a fact) would be that this is an example of an intermediate organism, and therefore evidence for evolution. However, the Christian interpretation (which is not a fact) would be that this is a unique organism that was created this way.

Each interpretation, however, is a result of the individual's ideology. Everyone's ideology influences how they see things, and how they think. It is not unscientific to believe that God created the world, when everything in the world is so beautifully and intricately organized. It is also not unscientific to think that organisms have evolved (changed over time, adapted, and reacted to selective pressure) when there is evidence that could be interpreted that way as well. True data are facts, it's the interpretation of data that is up to debate, and I think it's important to know the difference.

But back to the discussion of the balance. Don't you think, knowing the consequences of each viewpoint (atheism and Christianity) being true, that there would be more honest investigation into the scriptures for their message? It's astonishing to me that people are so quick to write off the Bible, so quick to disregard its claims, while also being fully aware that they cannot afford to be wrong.

To put this in perspective, try to imagine a situation where someone tells you that you owe ten thousand dollars to the government. You would probably think it was a scam, but you would at least investigate the claim thoroughly to make sure that you didn't actually owe any money. Because the last thing anyone wants is to be found guilty of a crime. Especially being found guilty against a governmental body, something that has the power to throw you in prison for the rest of your life.

The Bible is telling us the same thing, only the debt we owe God is something so big and spiritual that we cannot pay it back on our own. However, when God tells us about the crimes we have committed, and the debt we owe, we don't investigate the claim. We simply take an infinite level of skepticism towards the biblical text, and then write it off as being "unscientific."

Don't you think that we should actually investigate the claim thoroughly? You would think people would be 100% sure before they made such a drastic and eternal decision; on the contrary, we don't even investigate. That is why I want you to consider God's Word and our environment honestly, so that you may investigate for yourself if what the Bible has been saying for thousands of years is true.

Taking an infinite level of skepticism towards the Bible, by writing it off as false before you ever read it or study it, is only hurting your ability to understand it. And I think, considering the consequences of the different viewpoints being true, we should be as honest as possible when investigating the Bible.

I'm not saying that the fear of Hell should drive you to belief in something that you don't genuinely believe in; but I am saying that it should drive you to honest investigation.

Now, as we mentioned earlier, there are barriers for atheists that keep them from giving Christianity a chance or believing in God. These barriers are simply ideas and misconceptions about the Bible, God, and Christianity, that I believe stem mostly from popular opinion. In the chapters that follow, I will attempt to address the barriers that I believe keep people from coming to be Christians. As I address each of these barriers, my only request is that you give me your honest attention, and if you find my thoughts not to be very helpful then you are welcome to dismiss them.

11

CHRISTIANS

If Christians claim to be "transformed," and that they have the Spirit of God living inside of them, then why are they not perfect? Or at least, if they claim to be changed, why don't they look different than the rest of the world? These are the questions that people outside the church often are asking themselves; and to be honest, I've asked myself these questions many times. But concerning barriers for atheists, as we discussed in the last chapter, I believe this is one of the strongest. Atheists think about what Christianity apparently stands for: humility, honesty, love, generosity, sacrifice, forgiveness, salvation, grace, and mercy, but what they see from Christians is far from these ideals. I wouldn't even argue with them about that fact. So, they write off Christianity because to them, it doesn't really "work." Atheists see selfishness, self-righteousness, adultery, and pride from everyone who claims to be Christ followers. Therefore, one of the greatest barriers that keeps people outside the church from following Jesus, in my opinion, is that they do not see Christians living like Jesus did.

The reality though is that people outside the church are holding onto a misconception about Christianity. You see, Christianity does not claim to make people perfect on this side of heaven; it only claims to change their heart. What they do with that changed heart, often times, can be more reminiscent of their past self than who God has now empowered them to be. If Christianity was producing perfect people on this side of heaven, then there would be no room for the process of sanctification—which is a valuable process that, if you will allow me, I will explain further.

According to Orr (1915), sanctification can most literally mean "the state of proper functioning."[1] In the real world, for instance, if I were to sanctify a broken chair, then I would repair every broken piece until that chair could be used again— until it could be used for the intended purpose set for it by its designer. Therefore, when talking about our sanctification as Christians, we are being repaired so that we can be used for the intended purpose of The Great Designer. Or, as Tim Allen calls Him, The Builder; which I find a very fitting name when considering the example of the chair.

If Christians, after salvation, were made to be perfect "chairs" that could no longer mess up, then they would not have to lean on their designer for sanctification (or for further repair). This would create a very stagnant relationship between the chair and its designer—between God and man. One where the created thing would no longer have any reason to consult its Creator; because, after all, the created thing would be perfect without any more meddling by the One who fixed it in the first place.

While God does change a Christian at salvation, what happens is that the person now has the Holy Spirit living inside of their self, which allows one to have a deep and intimate relationship with God. What this does is it changes a person over time; it sanctifies them and sets them apart. They are not perfect the next day, but they begin to officially meet up with God every day, in prayer and in the study of the scriptures. These official meetings, however, are not the only encounters the Christian has with God. Since the Holy Spirit now resides in the Christian, he or she has permanent and constant communion with God; which maximizes their ability to be sanctified.

This Spirit inside of the Christian also leads them. He is a guiding force that must be felt whenever a follower of Christ makes a decision or faces a temptation. The Christian, however, can ignore the Spirit and His convictions. He or she can choose their own selfish desires over the desires of His Spirit; this is why Christians still have moments of lust, selfishness, self-righteousness, and pride. We still reside in a world of sin, and a world of choice. You see, you can take a man away from sin, but taking the sin out of man takes death. No matter how long someone has been sanctified by The Builder, so long as he or she is in this world of brokenness, they will always have the potential to mess up. There is always a chance they will fall.

Therefore, to put it simply, Christians are transformed and they still sin because they still have a free will to choose sin. However, the difference is that the transformed Christian now has the guiding Helper, the Holy Spirit, to lead them in the right direction and to give them power to resist temptation. If you are an atheist, and you're looking for a perfect Christian in order for you to believe in Jesus, then I'm sorry to tell you that you are looking for something that doesn't exist. To say that you are looking for a needle in a haystack would not be a good enough analogy; more appropriately, you are looking for a purple elephant in outer space.

Many things that atheists are looking for in order to believe are purple elephants in outer space—unrealistic ideas about what a true Christian should look like, or how a "true" God should manifest Himself to the world. I've heard from people before, "If only I found a Christian who actually lived like Jesus, then maybe I would believe in God." However, the Bible doesn't teach that Christians will live exactly like Jesus did. Not even the disciples followed God perfectly. They all, at some point, failed and betrayed Jesus.

Take Peter for example, he was a disciple of Jesus Christ, and yet he still denied Jesus three times. And not only did he deny Jesus, but he denied Him after Jesus had already warned him that he would do so. Peter, who we see in scripture sinning and denying the Savior of the world, is also the one we see answer Jesus' question (about who He is) in Mathew 16:16:

> Simon Peter replied, "You are the Christ, the Son of the living God." And Jesus answered him, "Blessed are you, Simon Bar-Jonah! For flesh and blood has not revealed this to you, but my Father who is in heaven. And I tell you, you are Peter, and on this rock I will build my church, and the gates of hell shall not prevail against it." (ESV)

Peter was not perfect, yet God the Father had revealed the truth of Jesus Christ to him. Peter's words declaring the truth of God's Son, Jesus, would be the very foundation of Jesus' church. We see this throughout scripture: followers of God who are not perfect, yet who are used greatly by Him. Often, these followers openly opposed God at some point in their life, even after they committed to following Him.

Another example of an imperfect follower of God is David. King David was said to be a man after God's own heart. Yet, David still committed adultery with Bathsheba, and he even had Bathsheba's husband, Uriah, killed. By definition David was a murdering adulterer. However, even after all of that nonsense and sin that he was caught up in, David was still continually used by God throughout his life, and God never abandoned him.

Therefore, it is not the case that scripture teaches us about perfect Christians. Rather, we see Christ followers who have high and low points, just like every person who follows Jesus today. What we do as Christians is we try our best to live like Jesus. He is our standard, but we understand that reaching that standard is impossible because Jesus was perfect and sinless, and we are broken and sinful. As long as we are on this side of heaven, we will not be fully repaired. Nevertheless, we should try our best to live like Jesus did, and we must rely on His Holy Spirit in order to do so.

One thing I am not advocating for is using your imperfectness as an excuse to sin, or to not follow Jesus. We are commanded to follow Christ and love God with everything we have. Not doing so is wrong and we will be held accountable for those actions. While we know that following Him perfectly is impossible, that does not give us an excuse not to try with all of our heart.

Concerning atheists who see this as a barrier to Christianity, or Christians who feel like they are not very good Christians, remember that the Bible doesn't even claim that Christians will be perfect on this side of Heaven. Whether you are looking at examples of people or theological passages, we are all broken sinners even after salvation; the only difference is we have Jesus living inside of us afterwards—which does mean that our life should look different than the world around us. Not that we should be perfect, of course, but that we will at least be set apart from the world through the process of sanctification.

Just like an onion, there are many layers to this discussion that we have not uncovered. One layer we haven't mentioned is the issue of people claiming to have Jesus in their heart who really don't. Unfortunately, that is the case for many people. Jesus tells us in Mathew 7: 14, "For the gate is small and the way is narrow that leads to life, and there are few who find it" (NASB). So there should be a small amount of people who will actually enter the gate that leads to life. But what we see is almost everyone claiming to be following the narrow path. Sadly, it must be the case that some people are not really on that path. I'm not going to say that anyone is—or is not—saved, but I will say that someone who has the Holy Spirit living inside of them will look different over time. And if you do not look different over time—if you do not bear good fruit—then there is good reason to evaluate your heart to see if you are really following the narrow path set before us.

Having Jesus in your heart is like having a professional construction man living in an old broken house. He is constantly walking around inside, finding cracks, broken beams, fallen roofs, and foundation issues. He may even find an idol stored away in an old closet. The first thing he'll do is talk to the owner of the house, and over time work with him to throw it away. He'll pick a structural problem, such as a fallen beam, and will begin working diligently to fix it. It's a lot of work for The Builder, and requires a lot of work by the owner of the old broken house as well. But over time, work is done and repairs are made. In simplest terms, The Builder cannot live inside of you for years without making any repairs, it is not in His character.

Therefore, with Jesus in your heart, your life will look different after years of cultivating a relationship with Him. I believe that many people who claim to have Jesus in their heart really don't, and this is another contributing factor to the false perception of Christians by atheists.

Also, it's not wise that we should compare Christians to non-Christians. More appropriately, we should compare a non-Christian only to himself after he becomes a Christian. Over time, if we see growth and a different kind of person develop, then we can conclude that we have found ourselves a genuine

Christian. After all, good trees do bear good fruit. And if our good God is living inside of someone, we can expect that person to bear more and more good fruit as that relationship blossoms.

You see, Christianity is more concerned with the difference in where particular people are when they come to Christ, and where those same people are at the end of their lives. If you are an atheist, then comparing a Christian to a non-Christian is not an accurate way to measure the effectiveness of the Christian faith.

I hope that we all, at the very least, can come to the understanding that no one is perfect, not even transformed Christians. Christians and atheists are *both* broken people. The only difference is that the Christian has begun to be repaired, while the atheist has not yet started. And if we were to say someone was better or worse, the Christian should be the first to disclose his end of the stick. He or she should be aware of the great measure of their own sinfulness.

Daniel Faucett

12

GOD AND TIME

One barrier that keeps people from becoming Christians is that they feel the Bible is inaccurate. I've noticed that people take a heightened level of skepticism towards it. It is not enough for people to question it with the same level of skepticism that they question other things. For the Word, they must take whatever level of skepticism is necessary in order to discount the claims made in it. For instance, people once claimed that King David never existed because there was no evidence for his existence found outside of the Bible. However, with the discovery of the Tel Dan Inscription, the biblical *and* historical figure was finally given credibility. Another example is how mainstream society claimed the Bible had been changed dramatically over the years. Then, to everyone's surprise, there was the discovery of the Dead Sea Scrolls (which were scrolls of Old Testament manuscripts). The significance of this discovery was that the manuscripts were around 1,000 years older than the previous oldest manuscripts used for biblical translations; to the world's surprise, there were no significant differences in the documents, indicating that the Bible had been transmitted through time with incredible accuracy. My point is this: We naturally raise this skepticism towards the Bible, yet with further investigation and discovery the Bible has been proven to be true and reliable. And if God did exist, this is exactly what we would expect to find from His divinely revealed Word.

For this chapter specifically, I want to focus on God and time, and how they reveal the perfect and authentic character of the Bible. There are many people in the world who try to discount what the Bible says about God and time because they operate on the preconception that God cannot exist. If God existing is not an option, then even the soundest evidence wouldn't make you consider the Bible as a reliable document. But if you operate on the preconception that God *can* exist (indicating that you have an understanding that everything is a possibility, just that some things are less likely than others), then we might gain some helpful knowledge about the subject of God and time. But first, before we get into the meat, we must establish that God is above time.

Obviously, if what the Bible has been saying for thousands of years is true, then God existed before time; which, by reason, makes God above time. Just like man is elevated above his created things, so is God above and outside of His.

FIGURE 12.1

If we use this circle to represent God, then we can imagine that He existed for an eternity before man was ever created—before time was ever created. I would like to speculate about what God was doing before He made time, but then again, it is impossible to even begin to think about actions, thoughts, or processes going on without three-dimensional space or time to measure the actions, thoughts, or processes of God. But, to feed our curiosity I must ask, what in the world was God doing before He made angels, man, Lucifer, time, or space? Could He have been drawing up plans for how He would reveal Himself? Or, perhaps He was spending careful time—which I shouldn't use the term *time* since it had not been invented yet—devising the laws of physics. Maybe He was articulating the appropriate flexibility in biological systems, and how much He would allow them to adapt in order to survive the variable conditions that He foreknew would take place on the Earth He was going to create. All this is just guesswork, though, at some point we must imagine the place at which God got bored of planning and actually made time and space and matter (represented by the straight line in the diagram).

FIGURE 12.2

This single line represents all of time (past, present, and future), as well as all physical space (and everything that takes up that physical space).

Once time and space and matter were created, there was finally a means to measure the passing of events. And, because there was space and matter and the creation week, there were also people to celebrate those events. There were birthdays, holidays, clocking in, and clocking out. Time specifically, since it is a created thing, must have a definite beginning and end like all formed things that do not possess a spirit, and must be in subjection to God—its Creator.

One thing that is interesting about created things is all of the relationships we find between them. Such as the relationship between the abiotic elements of Earth, and all of its biological life. Or the relationship between distant cosmological bodies and their gravitational pulls on near planets. And when it comes to time, the interesting thing is its relationship to space. You see, up until Albert Einstein came along, time was thought of as separate from space. Almost as if time was a completely separate concept—an abstract one. It was Einstein, however, who came up with the theory of special relativity—not to be confused with his later theory of general relativity. It was this theory of special relativity that connected the ideas of space and time into an interwoven continuum known as spacetime.

To explain this further, I want you to imagine a beam of light moving in the spacetime continuum at 299,792,548 meters per second. If you observed this beam moving in the night sky while you stood on planet Earth below, it would seem as if it were moving extremely fast. However, if you were able to fly off the surface of the Earth and catch up to the front of the beam of light, then you would be able to observe the light move as you moved alongside it. What you would discover is that the beam of light seems to be stationary when you are moving at the same speed. It's just like when you are driving 60 miles per hour down the interstate and another car is driving 60 miles per hour in the lane next to you. Relative to your own speed, it seems as though both cars are stationary, and that the world beneath you is sliding like a conveyor belt.

Now, I want you to imagine again that you are capable of travelling at the speed of light. You are in a desert with nothing but a brick wall behind you. This wall has a very large clock hanging on it. If you travelled away from the clock at the speed of light, then it would seem like time was not passing at all. This is because light must travel from the clock to your eye for you to register that time has passed; however, if you were moving at the speed of light then it would seem like time was not passing at all, or at least very slowly.

There was once an experiment performed with clocks and airplanes. It was known as the Hafele-Keating experiment. Essentially, Joseph Hafele and Richard Keating put an atomic clock on an airplane after calibrating it to be exactly similar to another clock that stayed stationary at the United States Naval Observatory (there were actually more clocks involved, but for the sake of simplicity, just imagine two). After the airplane flew around the world twice, they took the clock off the plane and compared it to the clock that had remained stationary. The clocks no longer agreed. It was a slight difference, but a measurable one. The difference was accurately predicted by special and general relativity. This reasserted the idea that when travelling at great speeds, your experience of time can be slowed. This shows that time is malleable, just like space, because what we are really experiencing is *spacetime*.

Another way I imagine spacetime is that to God it is like a long tunnel, and at every point in the tunnel there are pictures. When God comes to one point in the tunnel, He may see a series of pictures that are taken of the reader of this book. One picture is you picking it up, another is you reading it with your glasses on, and the last one is you putting the book down. Now, God can walk down the tunnel and simultaneously see snapshots of the reader of this book in the future, perhaps in your retirement years. Further down, your deathbed (sorry to be melancholic). He can see all the stages of everyone's life at the same time. It is in this tunnel, that all the snapshots of all people (past, present, and future) are already taken. At least, this is how I imagine it to be, and it would at least explain how God can see all time intervals simultaneously.

But you do see what we've done with these explanations, don't you? We've found that space and time are not separate; they are interwoven in something Einstein famously called spacetime. And it is this understanding of space and time that allows us to come to the realization that the most revolutionary discovery of space and time has actually pointed back to God. You see, if space and time are connected, then that means that our observations support the idea that God not only made space, but that He also made time. That we now can find the malleability of time and space and the interesting relationship between these two created things.

Another relationship Einstein discovered was in his *general* theory of relativity. This theory basically explains the relationship between occupied space and gravitational forces. This is simply another incredible connection between two created things. My only point with Einstein's theories are that they seem to reassert what the Bible has been saying about the origin of everything. Essentially, the idea that all things are created by God, and therefore should display characteristics of creation.

But enough on Einstein, let's move along with our diagram. I want you to focus on an event in the Bible; we can call it event "A". God not only sees what's happening in event A, but also in all other time intervals simultaneously because space and time are both His creation and under His control. How He does this I do not know, but if God was able to make time, then it's not too hard to imagine that He can take that knowledge of how it works, and use it to understand all things that are happening at all time intervals. Also, the important thing to know about event A is that God is not bound by the time interval in which the event occurs.

FIGURE 12.3

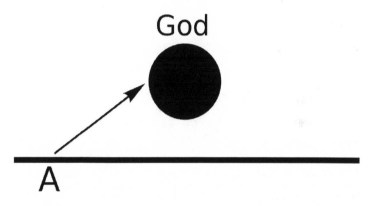

To God, I imagine it is like all events in human history are taking place at the same time (sort of like the tunnel we described earlier). Perhaps with one eye He sees Adam and Eve eating the fruit in the garden, and with the other He is viewing His crucifixion, and the down-the-road repercussions of the Holocaust. Not only this, but with a gazillion other eyes He can see all the infinite fractions of all time frames. This is another often forgotten concept: that each second can be divided into an infinite number of decimals or fractions that therefore can become their own little infinities. God can also see all these infinities that are made from the fractions of time frames. In a way, time is finite and infinite because there is a definite beginning and end, but the fractions can also be infinitely divided. But enough on these ideas, let's take it a step further.

FIGURE 12.4

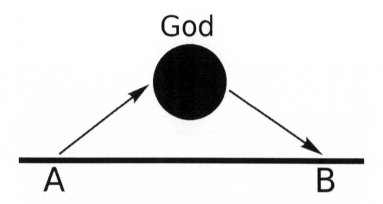

Let's say we have another event, event "B," that takes place in a later time interval. Since God is not bound by the time intervals He has created, but sees what's happening in each time interval at the same time, He is then able to supernaturally influence event A for the purpose of supernaturally revealing event B. What I am getting at is a roundabout way of viewing prophecy. If God does exist, then we would expect Him to be able to see future events. And when God influences someone in a current event, He could give them a clear revelation, or picture, of the future—because He can see the future as if it is happening at this very moment.

If you'll forgive me for the interruption, let me say that this—the idea that God can see the future as if it is happening right now—is why I believe, when the Bible talks about predestination, that sometimes it is talking about this ability of God to see all things happening at once. (Of course, I believe God predetermines things, but I also think He lets the sinful world choose sin, and that those choices still play into His great plan.) I don't think that God particularly wants certain people to go to Hell, for the Word tells us He wishes that none should perish, but that all should come to repentance (see 2nd Peter 3:9). However, God can see everything happening at every moment. With such a knowledge on people's actions (think back to our tunnel example), He knows full well who will go to heaven and who will not. He knows who will reject Him and who will accept Him. And when we start to raise the question, "But why doesn't God do more to alter the events so that more people will go to heaven?" we must consider what we're actually saying. You see, He is interweaving everything at all times, and as far as we can tell He has allowed some level of free will. What you think will help another person find God, may not actually help, and it may also be the case that God is considering other time frames and other people. Additionally, God could be simply allowing space for free will. God is working through every single person on this Earth simultaneously to interweave all of spacetime, and since every action that a person takes affects others, we must realize that there is a bigger picture at work. And when we find the root of this big picture, we will realize it is God's glory. All of time, space, matter, and human history will only point to this very thing.

But back to the main point. If God can see everything at all times, then He can give a person a very clear picture of the future. And if that someone was to write about that revelation, then we would expect it to not only come to pass, but in hindsight we would expect to see even the minute details explained accurately by that person. To explain biblical prophecy further, imagine that event A on our timeline is when the prophet, Isaiah, was moved to write Isaiah 53:5-12:

(5) But he was pierced for our transgressions; he was crushed for our iniquities; upon him was the chastisement that brought us peace, and with his wounds we are healed. (6) All we like sheep have gone astray; we have turned— every one—to his own way; and the Lord has laid on him the iniquity of us all. (7) He was oppressed, and he was afflicted, yet he opened not his mouth; like a lamb that is led to the slaughter, and like a sheep that before its shearers

is silent, so he opened not his mouth. (8) By oppression and judgement he was taken away; and as for his generation, who considered that he was cut off out of the land of the living, stricken for the transgression of my people? (9) And they made his grave with the wicked and with a rich man in his death, although he had done no violence, and there was no deceit in his mouth. (10) Yet it was the will of the Lord to crush him; he has put him to grief; when his soul makes an offering for guilt, he shall see his offspring; he shall prolong his days; the will of the Lord shall prosper in his hand. (11) Out of the anguish of his soul he shall see and be satisfied; by his knowledge shall the righteous one, my servant, make many to be accounted righteous, and he shall bear their iniquities. (12) Therefore I will divide him a portion with the many, and he shall divide the spoil with the strong, because he poured out his soul to death and was numbered with the transgressors; yet he bore the sin of many, and makes intercession for the transgressors. (ESV)

Even if you have barely heard of Jesus Christ, His life, or His crucifixion, you would still be able to understand who this passage is talking about. You would probably guess that this was a New Testament passage discussing the life of Jesus. However, contrary to what our reasoning would suggest, Isaiah 53 is in the Old Testament, and was written around 500 B.C. (Sarfati, 2011).[2] Which means that this was written around 500 years before Jesus Christ was ever born. And if you notice, the passage has a clear picture of what Jesus would do when He would come.

Therefore, we can say that event B is the life of Jesus in our diagram, and that event A is the prophecy of that event that was revealed to Isaiah.

If you focus on verse five specifically, you'll find that the person in the prophecy will be pierced for the transgressions of others; that His wounds would heal the wounds of others. Again, in verse twelve we find that not only will this person die for others, but that He will be "numbered with the transgressors." And, if you remember, Jesus was crucified next to two criminals. This paints a very clear picture for us—even more so in hindsight—because Jesus would die on the Cross for the salvation and healing of the human race.

Verse twelve also indicates that this person will make "intercession for the transgressors." If you know anything at all about Jesus or Christianity, then you know that this could not be a truer statement about the future. Jesus came to make intercession on behalf of believers. He has come to mediate the relationship between God and man. If you remember, after Jesus was crucified, Mark 15:38 tells us that "The curtain of the temple was torn in two from top to bottom" (NIV). This curtain, or *veil* as some translations word it, was in the holy temple in Jerusalem, and was symbolic of man's separation from God because of God's immense holiness. The veil literally separated the earthly dwelling place of God's presence from the earthly dwelling place of man's. This curtain showed humanity that we were not righteous; that we could not be in God's presence. Therefore, when the veil was torn it signified that Christ had bridged this barrier, that He could now make us righteous, and mediate our relationship with God. If you focus on verse eleven, "by his knowledge shall the righteous one, my servant, make many to be accounted righteous." This is also powerfully correct in that Jesus makes us righteous by being the sacrifice for our sins.

It's interesting, with the diagram in mind, what this reveals to us about God and time. It clarifies how Isaiah could have explained the coming Savior so accurately. If God can see all things happening at once (perhaps with a spacetime tunnel), then it is no surprise that these prophecies came to fruition. Isaiah must have been revealed a portion of this spacetime tunnel because he even got the minute details right in his prophecy: for instance, that the coming Messiah would not open his mouth. This was fulfilled, if you recall, when Christ was being falsely accused of crimes in front of the high priest. According to Mathew 26:62-63, "Then the high priest stood up and said to Jesus, 'Are you not going to answer? What is this testimony that these men are bringing against you?' But Jesus remained silent" (NIV). If the Bible were not true, and if God did not exist, then we wouldn't expect someone to be able to describe the life of a person coming in the future with so much accuracy. We would expect to find something wrong with the prophecy, something in the details. However, what we find is that Isaiah writes about Jesus as if he saw Jesus' life himself. As if Isaiah saw Jesus keeping His mouth closed, dying for the sins of others, and being the mediator for man to communicate freely with God.

Approximately in A.D. 90, the Gospel of John clarified this point for us when he said the following, "Isaiah said these things because he *saw* [my emphasis] his glory and spoke of him." (John 12:41; ESV). John was referring to Isaiah's prophecies concerning the coming Messiah. This verse specifically was in reference to when Jesus rode into Jerusalem on a donkey, and when many of the people refused to believe in Him even after He had raised Lazarus from the dead. So it is clear that Isaiah had been given a visual of Jesus' life. Otherwise, his prophecy would not have been articulated so appropriately, and he would not have gotten the details right.

Of course, we can raise the question that perhaps the people who wrote the fulfillment of the prophecy could have lied about the events to make it seem like they were fulfilled. After all, the people who wrote the New Testament must have been aware of the Old Testament prophecies. This is a good, appropriate, and critical question to ask. Unfortunately for the biblical skeptic, this prophecy can be reasserted by another writer at the time, Cornelius Tacitus. Tacitus was a secular writer who reasserted that Jesus lived, died on the Cross, and that He had an incredible impact. His writings help us to have confidence in our conclusion that this prophecy was genuinely fulfilled. We know Tacitus at least was not biased towards Christianity—as the writers of the Gospels would have been. Tacitus literally thought that Christians were crazy. He refers to their belief in the resurrection as superstitious (Kirby, 2017).[3] Thankfully, there are many other reliable sources that reassert the authenticity of Jesus' existence and fulfillment of this prophecy.[38]

The incredible thing about Isaiah 53, though, is that most people (even non-Christians) believe that Jesus existed and died on the Cross. If we believe those things, why can't we take it a slight step further and believe that Jesus did not open His mouth in the courts? Or that Jesus claimed to be God? It's a simple step forward to buy into the other aspects of Jesus' fulfillment of prophecy.

And not only do we have secular support for some of what this prophecy is talking about, but we also have the New Testament—an important fact that I think we are too quick to ignore—that testifies exactly to what this prophecy is talking about. The four gospels were written by eyewitnesses of Jesus, people who knew Him face-to-face. These eyewitnesses who wrote about Jesus would not have risked their lives to write about Him if they did not have the truth. But these accounts are ignored because materialists refuse to acknowledge a supernatural power as a root source of prophecy and prophecy fulfillment.

In summary, by reading this prophecy we can begin to visualize the reality of God's dominion over time, and how God has used time to reveal Himself. We find that God—in order to be able to accurately predict the future and influence the present—must be able to see all time intervals simultaneously, and therefore must be omniscient. Whether He has a spacetime tunnel full of snapshots is uncertain, but it at least allows us to visualize how He may see things. Concerning atheists and their barriers to Christianity, I believe that considering the Bible and its prophecy is one of the best ways to begin to see Christianity as a viable world perspective. While this simple example does not prove that God is real, it should provoke your thoughts, and perhaps it will give you a reason to investigate further.

13

THE TELEOLOGICAL ARGUMENT

If you have taken any biology course, then you have probably heard of *Darwinism* (or Darwinian evolution, or Darwinian theory). The idea that organisms change over time as a result of changes in heritable physical or behavioral traits (Than, 2015).[4] Changes that result in an organism being better adapted to its environment; with a better ability to survive, and a higher chance of producing a greater number of offspring (Than, 2015).[4] These offspring that are more fit are then selected for, which is called *natural selection*. Over the course of millions of years, this process is said to account for the origin of biological structures found on our planet. This is the dominant theory for explaining the origin of new cellular systems: essentially that mutations on offspring are selected for when beneficial. The mutations and variations in offspring that are negative are not selected for because these organisms are less likely to reproduce and propagate their DNA.

Microevolution vs. Macroevolution

Before I move forward, let me establish what I mean when I use the word *evolution* in this chapter. I do not simply mean small, observable changes. These small observable changes would reside in the category of *microevolution*. This definition of evolution is irrefutable and has been observed in the present day. There is no refuting certain animals have been bred down into different breeds of the same kind of animal, and that humans have gotten taller (and more cancerous) over time. Or that mountains have grown higher during the time interval in which you were sipping on some coffee this morning. No Christian has a problem accepting microevolution, these undeniable facts can be observed and measured as they are happening. However, when I use the word evolution in this chapter, I really mean molecules-to-man evolutionary theory—otherwise known as *macroevolution*. From abiogenesis to a thriving, creative, and loving human being. Macroevolution must be accepted by anyone claiming that natural processes resulted in mankind over a long period of time. However, because this definition of evolution requires billions of years, it cannot be observed in the present day. Therefore, in order to support macroevolution, we must look to evidence in the past and make interpretations; or we can look at structures in our current environment, and see if it was possible for them to have arisen by numerous, slight modifications over time. Nonetheless, since these changes from molecules to human beings cannot be observed as they are happening, we have to look to the past to draw these conclusions, and that process comes with a lot of room for uncertainty. (This is why it is called the *theory* of evolution and not the *law* of evolution.)

One major problem with macroevolutionary theory is its starting point. The simplest organism that all life is said to have evolved from is the *amoeba*. (Of course, not the exact amoeba we have today, but a very similar ancestral amoeba that resembles the one we have today.) The problem with this hypothesis is that the amoeba is extremely complicated. Even Richard Dawkins, a devout atheist, acknowledges that one single amoeba contains the information equivalent to 1,000 complete sets of the *Encyclopedia Britannica*.[39] This means that if you wrote the amoeba's DNA code down on paper, with every A, T, G, and C accounted for, it would fill the pages of 1,000 encyclopedias. What's most impressive of all is that those letters would actually mean something; they are the amoeba's biological blueprints.

I want you to imagine that you are walking in the woods one Fall afternoon, and you find a large book resting in the leaves. Would you conclude that this book came from natural, unintelligent processes? Of course not. You would assume that an intelligent person wrote that book. But what if you found a stack of 1,000 books? Your conclusion of design and intelligence would be even more supported. To make it even more interesting, what if after you read the books, you found that they were all part of a massive anthology? Your conclusion of design and purpose would be irrefutable at this point.

To take it one more step (if you are not already convinced of design), what if you found a massive temple in the woods, and inside there were these same books, but each book contained information on how to build the temple they reside in? Not only do you have the information overload indicating design, but you also have the building associated with the blueprints. Your conclusion of design would again be irrefutable.

The amazing thing about biology is that this scenario is exactly what we find. In nature, we find that the first organism has an incredible architecture, *and* highly intelligent blueprints. With this evidence, it's not illogical to consider the possibility of an architect. (Especially when you consider that there is no evidence to suggest that an information system can come from natural, unintelligent processes; a point which Behe makes quite clear in *Darwin's Black Box*.)

Therefore, I think the first major problem for macroevolution is its most fundamental premise: that 1,000 encyclopedias worth of information came from natural, unintelligent processes. This amount of sophisticated information is too large to be accounted for by natural processes.

The second problem for macroevolution is that the information we do find in nature codes for workers who can read the blueprints themselves. These workers are coded for by the very DNA that tells the workers how to create the biological structures! So not only do you have blueprints that tell you how the building will look, but you also have blueprints that tell you how to build the very workers who will build the building.

The naturalist clearly has a dilemma. Which came first, the workers or the blueprints? If you say the blueprints (DNA) came first, then how would anything get built without the workers (factors) already there from the beginning? A blueprint thrown on top of rocks doesn't make a stone house. You have to have someone there to put the pieces together. Not to mention that you have to summon materialistic faith to believe that the blueprints came about by natural processes in the first place.

If you say the workers came first, then how would they

know what to build without directions? Hiring construction men is pointless if they have no blueprint to go by. Not to mention that you have to have materialistic faith to believe that the workers came about by natural processes in the first place.

We have a classic "which came first, the chicken or the egg?" dilemma. I think both dilemmas are better solved by the theory of Intelligent Design than by the theory of macroevolution.

Law vs. Theory

A law is an undeniable and observable fact. If you operate under the definition that evolution is simply change over time, then evolution would be a law because it would be an undeniable and observable fact—everything changes over time, and these changes can be observed. This law of evolution would be synonymous with the law of gravity set forth by Isaac Newton—which is an undeniable and observable fact that everyone can see and accept. In contrast to a law, a theory is the *explanation* of the observational data. It's like a super-hypothesis. Since the hypothesis of evolution (molecules becoming man over time) holds somewhat well when interpreting data from the past, it is accepted as a theory. It is a good explanation of the data, but it is not the only one we can value, and it has exceptions where the theory makes little sense and cannot be applied.

In order for molecules-to-man evolutionary theory to be valid, we have to be able to explain structures found in the environment with evolutionary mechanisms: descent with genetic differences, mutations, genetic drift, migration (gene flow), long periods of time, and natural selection. I know we can explain how many organisms obtained certain structures and abilities through evolutionary mechanisms, such as when a bacterium accepts a plasmid and gains a new ability; nevertheless, this does not explain how the plasmid came into existence in the first place. Evolutionary theory must explain how these structures (such as the plasmid) came into existence in the first place, and it must be through evolutionary mechanisms. The problem with evolution is not in the transferring of structures, breeding, genetic shuffling, or even in slight modifications of a structure that already works; the problem is in the details of how a structure that works came into existence in the first place. The great task of the creationist is to explain how it is more likely that the first form of these structures were created.

Darwin's Day

When Darwin published his famous work, *The Origin of Species*, in 1859, little was known about what was inside the cell. The state of technology and experimentation at the time limited our understanding. (Think about it, the American Civil War would not start for another two years. And during that time people were unsure how to treat simple infections.) This primitive scientific understanding considered, we couldn't say much about the cell beyond it being a glob of protoplasm that performed functions via unknown mechanisms. The actual structures and abilities inside the cell were a complete mystery. Microtubule assemblage and dismantling, the mitochondrion's power-generating ability, DNA coding for RNA, RNA coding for proteins, ribosomes, intracellular transport, the packaging ability of the Golgi, dynein and kinesin motors, and many other characteristics of the cell not mentioned here were yet to be understood.

With that said, what scientists were able to accomplish in the past is tremendous and should not be discredited. Nor should they be viewed as less than those who do science today. One can only do the best with what he is given. I think the scientists of the past should be seen as super intelligent heroes. In other words, I would consider the two men who invented calculus, Isaac Newton and Gottfried Leibniz, to be more intelligent than the men and women who can simply apply calculus to new situations. It takes a special kind of mind to discover and invent, rather than simply to learn and apply.

I say all this to make the point that Darwin was intelligent, ahead of his time, and his theory on the origin of species was revolutionary; however, he did not have an accurate understanding of the way things worked form a cellular and biochemical perspective. He could not possibly have understood the structure of a bacterial flagellum, intracellular transport, or the proteins involved in blood clotting. Our understanding of these things came about long after Darwin's theory of evolution by natural selection was given. While his theory makes sense when looking at large structures from a *micro*evolutionary perspective, such as with Darwin's finches, his theory begins to become questionable when looking at biology from a cellular and biochemical perspective.

Darwin, completely ignorant of cellular mechanisms and biochemistry, once wrote in *The Origin of Species* (1859):

> If it could be demonstrated that any complex organ existed which could not possibly have been formed by numerous, successive, slight modifications, my theory would absolutely break down.[5]

Of course, Darwin goes on to say that he has not found any such example. However, if someone happened to find an example of a biological organ, system, or cascade, that could not have arisen by slight modifications over time, then we would have a good reason to doubt his theory. After all, science has come a long way since 1859, perhaps someone has discovered such an example. And if we did find an example of a structure in the biological world that could not have arisen purely by natural processes, then one is forced to acknowledge that Darwin's theory does not explain the origin of everything we find in nature. It doesn't necessarily mean that the God of the Christian Bible made the structure in question, it just means the structure likely did not come about by numerous, successive, slight modifications over time. And if it did not come about in this fashion, then perhaps it was the product of some form of Intelligent Design. Whose intelligence is another question altogether.

Bias

I think it's relevant to note that this area of science (looking into the origin of things) is where our biases come into play. I'm a Christian, so obviously I have a multitude of biases when looking at issues such as marriage, abortion, debt, or science. However, I will admit that my biases come from the Word and my relationship with the Creator. God is the lens by which I look at everything, including biological systems. In contrast, naturalists often will not admit their biases. They claim they have a completely unbiased approach to science because they exclude God from the equation. However, in excluding God as an option for the explanation of phenomenon, they are admitting their bias. They are biased because they refuse to acknowledge Intelligent Design as a source of explanation, even if the data points in that direction.

Of course, you can be biased and still be right. Just because a naturalist is biased doesn't mean he's wrong. Likewise, just because a religious person is biased doesn't mean he's wrong either.

Furthermore, just because someone is religiously motivated doesn't mean they're wrong. You could be 100% religiously motivated by the Bible and still be completely right in your assertions. However, when your biases get in the way of following the data where it leads is when science has a problem; and this problem goes both ways.

Simply calling ourselves an atheist or a Christian pushes us into corners full of biases and beliefs—whether our particular corner has evidence to support its claims does not account for all of the biases present. The Christian has biases that are not backed by any evidence, and so does the naturalist. I guess if you desire to be completely unbiased, then you shouldn't hold any beliefs or views that extend beyond accepted fact.

For example, the Christian should not believe that angels or demons exist. The Christian takes this aspect of Christianity by faith in the eyewitness accounts from past generations, and from their apparent influence in the present day. Additionally, the naturalist should not believe in the spontaneous generation of the first lifeform, or any naturalistic explanation on the origin of the universe (such as the multiverse theory). These views from the naturalist are just as religious as the Christian ideas of demons and angels. However, the Christian view is at least attested to by eyewitness accounts from the past, rather than by speculation from the present.

You see, for both Christians and atheists, there is something that pushes us beyond the facts. The atheist can pull out as many facts, arguments, or philosophies as he wants to, but at some point he will run out of them. The same goes for the Christian. At some point the facts have to run out, and that's when our biases take over and we just say what we believe.

I think it is a spiritual force for both Christians and atheists that drives us beyond the facts. If it were not for a spiritual force (or some force beyond objective fact that gives us bias), then why should we go beyond the facts at all? If there are no outside forces at play, then shouldn't we reach the end of an argument, and whoever runs out of facts first be completely convinced by the other person? But this isn't how the world works. People are stubborn and hard-headed—myself most of all. We lose arguments, yet we still hold onto our beliefs and biases. We have *faith* that there are more facts, arguments, and philosophies out there to support our beliefs—even when the evidence (or at least our awareness of it) is lacking at the moment. So, I think there is something beyond mere fact that holds onto us and pushes us, and I believe in many cases this is a spiritual force.

These spiritual forces are trying to push everyone into one

of the only two corners: *with* Christ or *against* Christ. There are no other options. I think that the facts themselves are only a mirage, or a mask, of the spiritual world. Each person is spiritually led, and the spirit—whether Holy or evil—inside of themselves presupposes interpretations of the facts. This is why the Christian goes beyond the facts, the Holy Spirit leads his way beyond the evidence into action. A Christian cannot prove completely that Christ performed miracles, he or she has faith that He performed them beyond the evidence present.

The naturalist may not admit it, but they also are influenced by a spiritual force that pushes them to have faith in evolution and natural processes even when the evidence is not there (as you will see with those who believe in the *multiverse theory*). The naturalist just doesn't call it faith. However, the spiritual force influencing them in their faith is very powerful, as we have discussed many times in this book. And that spiritual force results in just as much bias and motivation to move beyond the facts as the force that is influencing the Christian.

But for the sake of science and the pursuit of truth, we must set aside our biases and honestly take a look at where the data is pointing. Perhaps some things point to an intelligent designer. If we are too consumed with our biases, we will never see it even if it is there. The same goes for the Christian, because many things point to Darwinian evolution as a plausible origin explanation. We must set aside our biases when looking at nature, at least for a moment, so we can recognize whether something in question was a product of design or a product of evolution.

For instance, we cannot deny that certain breeds of dog are the product of evolution. To say that all dog breeds were created would be a biased claim from a creationist who refuses to acknowledge the facts. The evidence clearly points to the fact that dogs have evolved into their various breeds. But, to say that the very first dogs were a product of design is an entirely different claim (this claim is actually more in alignment with scripture, and better backed by the evidence). Intelligent design enthusiasts should be more concerned with the latter.

Irreducible Complexity

But back to the main point. Can Darwinian evolution explain everything we find in nature? Michael Behe is a biochemical researcher and professor at Lehigh University, and he has pursued an answer to this very question. Behe has popularized the term *irreducible complexity* to make his case against Darwinism. Behe defines Irreducible complexity in his work, *Darwin's Black Box*. My simplified definition for the reader is this: there are some biochemical structures whose complexity cannot be reduced. In other words, there are some things we find in nature that are so complicated and interdependent that their structure cannot be simplified. The removal of any part of the structure renders the system as a whole useless (or nonfunctional). Can you see why this concept could pose a problem for Darwinian theory? Evolution demands physical precursors that actually function—otherwise the precursors would never have evolved in the first place. If there are no possible physical precursors to an existing structure, then perhaps there are none. When there are no precursors, it is reasonable to conclude the structure did not evolve from a primordial form. If it did not evolve by slight modifications over a long period of time, then an alternative explanation is necessary. I believe the likely alternative explanation to be that the separate parts were assembled at one time. And I believe that the parts were assembled by the intervention of an intelligent designer.

It's not that we can say for sure that God is the source of the intelligent assembling and design that we observe, but regardless, intelligence must have been involved to form many of the intricate, irreducibly complex structures in nature. Needless to say, Behe uses the mousetrap in his renowned book to explain irreducibly complex systems. I will try to summarize the mousetrap example in as simplest terms as possible.

A mousetrap contains five different parts that are all necessary to catch mice: wooden platform, spring, hammer, holding bar, and a catch.[6] Every one of these parts are required to catch mice. For instance, if you remove the catch, you will not be able to catch mice. Or if you remove the spring, the catch will not have a force that will hold the mice. If you remove the wooden platform, the individual pieces will be useless concerning the function of the entire system, because they will not be held together properly. Each part of this system is necessary to accomplish its function: to catch mice. This is a great example of an irreducibly complex system because the complexity of the instrument as a whole cannot be reduced without removing the function of the entire system.

Of course, there are scenarios where the individual pieces themselves could have served purposes. For example, the platform could have served as a spacer for an unbalanced desk. The spring could have served as a tension force on a car seat. Likewise, the other pieces in the mousetrap could also have served other, independent purposes. However, if these pieces were surviving by serving entirely independent functions, then there would be no reason for these parts to come together at one instance in order to accomplish a completely alternative function (to catch mice). Unless, an intelligent source went out and found all of the components, and then altered them to where they would fit together perfectly (by adding holes, adhesives, slots, and adjusting the size and shape of each piece). Then, these pieces would fit together to meet the function that a designer clearly had in mind.

In contrast to Intelligent Design, evolution demands functioning physical precursors to the *system*—not the individual pieces. In the case of the mousetrap, there are none. The logical conclusion here is that an intelligent source created and designed the mousetrap. In this case, I don't think anyone disagrees on the fact of Intelligent Design. However, what about when it comes to even more complicated, interdependent biological systems?

The bacterial flagellum, an microbiological tail-looking apparatus, is one such example of exquisite natural complexity.[8] The bacterial flagellum has an outstanding resemblance to an outboard motor (see Figure 13.1). Flagella contain a rotor, stator, hook, drive shaft, motor, filament, rings, and other working parts that allow it to function as an organ. The function is exactly similar to the function of an outboard motor: to propel movement through water. When it comes to the biological motor, however, there are forty different protein parts that are required to make this bacterial flagellum function.

Howard Berg, a Harvard biophysicist, has called this the most efficient machine in the universe.[9] And rightfully so, a vibrio cell's flagellum has been clocked at 100,000 rotations per minute (Francis, Sosinsky, Thomas, & DeRosier, 1999).[7] To put this in perspective, modern automobiles usually operate between 1,500 and 2,000 rotations per minute. So this biological machine is operating at a faster rate by a factor of 50. Not only is it fast, but it's also extremely quick. It only takes a quarter turn for this machine to stop its rotations; then, it can start back spinning in the other direction in a split second. It's incredibly efficient, and undeniably complex. Even the angle that the flagellum is curved is significant and coded for in the DNA sequence.

FIGURE 13.1

BACTERIAL FLAGELLUM: AN ARTIST'S RENDITION

If any part of this machine was removed, the organ would lose its function. Resulting in an inactive flagellum that would be a hindrance for the organism. For instance, if you removed the filament, then there would be nothing to grip and paddle through the water; the organism would not be able to propel itself, and would not be selected for. If you removed the hook, then perhaps the angle at which the flagellum would spin would be too low to grip water. If you removed the motor, then there would be no energy to power the structure. If you merely reduced the supply of energy, then perhaps the structure would not turn fast enough to function properly. A boat motor that only turns one rotation per minute doesn't get you anywhere, and neither does a flagellum with low energy. There are many other scenarios not mentioned here that could pose problems for Darwinism when applied to this specific biological structure.

This begs the question: could this highly sophisticated structure have arisen through natural selection and small modifications over time? It's not likely, because this structure is irreducibly complex, just like the mousetrap—which could not have arisen by small modifications over time either. Any primordial form to the mousetrap (that is missing one of the finished structure's parts) would be completely useless in catching mice. Similarly, any possible primordial form to the bacterial flagellum is very likely to be useless also.

The type III secretion system (T3SS), a similar microbiological machine that secretes toxins, has been used to explain the evolution of the flagellum. The only problem with this explanation is that the flagellum seems to be the more ancient device (according to phylogeny).[40] You can't say that the flagellum came from the secretory system if the flagellum came first. This is sort of like saying that someone's son is also their father, it's a biological impossibility. My son will never be my biological father.

Keep in mind I'm not saying Darwinian evolution can't explain other structures found in nature, I'm just saying it doesn't provide a satisfactory explanation for this particular structure.

Another example of irreducible complexity is the blood clotting cascade (or blood coagulation) found in animals. It is the complicated cascade that is responsible for keeping animals from bleeding to death when they are cut open. (A cascade is simply a series of events where one thing leads to another.) If it were not for the presence of the complete process of blood coagulation in organisms with circulatory systems, a simple cut could cause an organism to bleed to death. This can be seen in individuals with moderate to severe *haemophilia*.

Obviously, this process is necessary for survival, but how does it work?

Blood coagulation simply makes the blood turn from a liquid substance to a gel-like substance. It does this through two different avenues. There is an extrinsic pathway (which occurs due to outside tissue damage) and there is an intrinsic pathway (which occurs due to trauma in the actual blood); both lead to a clot. When blood coagulation occurs, usually both of these pathways are working simultaneously.

FIGURE 13.2

COAGULATION CASCADE WITHOUT REGULATION

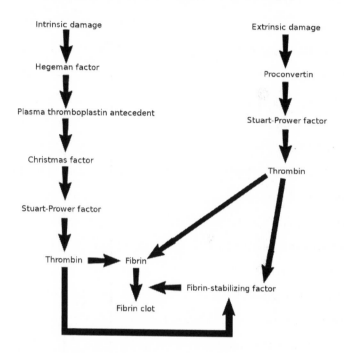

When intrinsic trauma occurs, Hegeman factor is activated (see diagram). Activated Hegeman factor then activates plasma thromboplastin antecedent; which activates Christmas factor; which activates Stuart-Prower factor; which converts prothrombin (not shown) to thrombin; which converts fibrinogen (not shown) to fibrin. Thrombin also activates fibrin-stabilizing factor, and fibrin-stabilizing factor converts fibrin into cross-linked fibrin clots. The extrinsic pathway is similar, and from the diagram I think you can see how they both interrelate and could function simultaneously in the event of trauma.

It is important to note that this is a grossly over-simplified version of the blood clotting cascade. In the diagram, I have reduced the number of factors present significantly, and I have left out one of the most important parts to this intricate system: regulation. If this process was allowed to run the direction shown in the diagram without ever stopping, then the clot would get bigger and bigger until it completely stopped blood flow. The result would be death of the organism due to over clotting of the blood. Therefore, the actual process is much more complicated than this and involves many other factors. These other factors regulate this process by inactivating proteins involved at various steps in the clotting cascade (antithrombin, protein C, etc.). The point being that this diagram does not do the complexity of the system justice. However, since Intelligent Design enthusiasts usually try to over complicate things, I have resisted the urge. I have given a simple diagram to make the point that the general pathway is still irreducibly complex. (The argument for design in this case is so strong that I think it can make due with a general pathway.)

Nevertheless, it is no argument that this process is complicated, but is it irreducibly complex? I would say yes, because all of the factors involved in the blood coagulation process have a purpose and are necessary for blood clotting to occur. Without one of the intermediate factors, the process would not be successful in stopping blood flow at an area of injury. Without the regulatory proteins, perhaps the clot would never stop forming. Both scenarios result in serious complications. My conclusion is that this cascade could not have arisen by means of numerous, slight modifications over time. This means that this entire process would have to be assembled at one instance.

To illustrate my point further, I want you to imagine that you walk into a thick Alabama forest on a hot summer day. You cut your way through the thick forest for about thirty minutes. Just when you are about to turn back from exhaustion, you swing your machete one last time. Suddenly, you feel the resistance give way. You find yourself fall forward into a circular clearing of recently cut grass in the forest. A near perfect circle. In the middle of the groomed grass is a high pile of grainy feed. You eat some of the grain and begin to wish you brought water along with you.

Now, in this situation, would you assume that this clearing in the woods came about by numerous, successive, slight modifications over time? Of course not. The fact that it is all naturally occurring items (grass, grain, trees) is not relevant to your conclusion. You would assume that someone cleared the circular spot in the woods, and put grain down in order to accomplish a specific purpose. There was an *intervention* with nature. (They were probably trying to attract an animal.) So, in this example we find an assemblage of different factors (cleared grass, cleared trees, and grain) put together for a specific purpose: to attract an animal. All of which were fueled by an intelligent source that monkeyed with natural resources.

However, to more appropriately explain the blood coagulation process, I want you to imagine again that you are walking into a thick Alabama forest. This time you stumble upon a catapult in the middle of a large, cleared field full of short sticks in the ground. You sit down on the catapult in a state of wonder when, all of a sudden, it launches a metal ball. The ball soars through the sky. It eventually lands with a thud in a large funnel across the clearing. The ball spirals down the funnel until it drops straight down onto a wooden arm. The arm gently swings the ball to a waterwheel. The waterwheel turns until the ball falls directly onto a wooden track. The track carries the ball towards you as it gains momentum moving downward. The ball, now with great speed, launches up a small incline in the track and soars through the air over your head. (It reflects the sunlight into your eyes, temporarily blinding you!) At the end of its skyward course, and after you have regained your vision, the ball hits a small stick in the ground next to you. This stick falls down onto another stick, causing a domino effect of many other small sticks until you realize that the sea of sticks that filled the entire clearing are now all laying down. However, just when you think that the charade is over, the last stick to fall hits a rope on a nearby tree. This rope begins to be pulled by a weight on its opposite side. You notice that the rope is attached to all of the sticks, and slowly but surely the rope (being pulled by some unseen weight), pulls up all of the sticks that were laying down in the field. Now, each stick is standing upright. In wonder and confusion you sit back down on the catapult. All of a sudden, the catapult launches another metal ball and the process starts all over.

When it comes to the blood-clotting cascade, we find the very same thing as we mentioned in this second scenario. We find something in the tropical happenstance of nature that severely stands out. We find not just a circular clearing, or an assemblage of parts; we find a *cascade* of multiple factors that are present for a specific purpose: to keep you from bleeding to death when you experience trauma. And not only do we have the factors that keep you from bleeding to death, but we also have the regulation of the process that keeps you from dying from a clot (as represented by the rope that pulled all of the sticks upright at the end).

When we find something in nature that resembles this level of complexity and purpose, it is not illogical to conclude design. It's sort of like finding a Rube-Goldberg machine in nature; the logical conclusion is design.

It's funny that we use a completely different kind of reasoning when we look at things in nature than we do when we look at things assembled by man. Why do we look at the organization of a watch differently than the organization of the blood-clotting cascade, or the bacterial flagellum? All of these clearly represent design, yet when our reasoning crosses over to things in nature the conclusions drawn are disregarded.

I should make note that nature operates differently than watches. Biological systems have metabolism and self-regulation, whereas mechanical systems are usually reliant on human maintenance and input. However, both biological and mechanical machines can work in extremely similar ways. We can see this especially in the case of the bacterial flagellum and an outboard motor. Both resemble each other in structure and function. So when we find a bacterial flagellum in nature, it is really like finding an outboard motor made of purely biological constituents. In so doing, it is not faulty reasoning to detect Intelligent Design in both cases—especially when you consider the mechanisms involved in the machines under study, and how they each may be irreducibly complex.

However, an obvious dissention occurs here in the explanation of the blood-clotting cascade phenomenon. The naturalist would attempt to explain this system via solely natural processes, and the creationist would explain it from the viewpoint of an intelligent source monkeying with nature. However, there is a huge problematic question for the naturalist: How did all the parts get together in a step-by-step fashion? This is a cascade, which means we need the precursor factor to activate the next factor in the series. This happens so on and so forth until we form an actual clot. If you remove an intermediate factor the whole process shuts down and you bleed to death. (Just like in our catapult-in-the-forest example, if you removed the funnel from across the field, then the ball would land in the dirt and the sticks would never get knocked down.) On the other hand, if you do not have regulation of this coagulation process, then every organism would have heavy blood clots (the sticks would never be pulled upright). This means that you have to have the entire cascade leading to a clot, and the process of regulation, all come together at one instance. Additionally, you would have to have all of this in place *before* a circulatory system could even develop. Why would a cascade like this be selected for before a circulatory system existed?

Even if you took a primordial, low blood pressure system—such as the one Kenneth Miller once suggested— there are still roadblocks at every evolutionary advancement. Whenever you add something to the system to increase blood clotting (such as a protease), without regulation of that protease it could be detrimental. The addition of a weak protease is not necessarily an evolutionary advantage either. Miller writes in the draft of his book, *Finding Darwin's God* (keep in mind this excerpt was removed by the editor and was not actually in the official book, but Miller reaffirmed his support of this excerpt in an online article):

> But just as soon as the occasional clot becomes large enough to present health risks, natural selection would favor the evolution of systems to keep clot formation in check. And where would these systems come from? From pre-existing proteins, of course, duplicated and modified. The tissues of the body produce a protein known as alpha-1-antitrypsin which binds to the active site of serine proteases found in tissues and keeps them in check. So, just as soon as clotting systems became strong enough, gene duplication would have presented natural selection with a working protease inhibitor that could then evolve into antithrombin, a similar inhibitor that today blocks the action of the primary fibrinogen-cleaving protease, thrombin.[31]

I see a few problems with Miller's statements. For one, if the clot became large enough to cause "serious health risks," then the organism's clotting system would not be selected for advancement in regulation of clotting, but it is more likely to be selected for a reduction in the clotting that is causing the problem. In this scenario, the clotting factors that once served the purpose of helping the organism form clots, should now be selected for reduction to the simpler system that once served its purpose well. In other words, why would you hike a mountain when it is easier to walk through a valley?

I think it is more likely to select for a simpler system, especially if it is fewer evolutionary steps (which it would be in this case). Selecting for the beginnings of a regulatory system does not seem to fit the picture of likely natural advancements for survival. The reality is that the organism needs to survive, and it needs to right now, so natural selection would select for the shortest and most likely path to survival—which I believe to be a reduction in the system's clotting ability, rather than advancements towards a regulatory system which includes a protease inhibitor. (Not to mention that a mutated SERPINA1 gene—the gene that codes for alpha-1-antitrypsin—can result in non-functional proteins that accumulate in the liver, causing a form of infantile cirrhosis.) Naturalists often presuppose evolutionary advancements, even when natural selection is more likely to select for reductions that better fit the immediate survival needs of the population's offspring. Think about it, who is more likely to survive: an organism with serious blood clots and non-working pre-regulatory factors, or an organism with a simpler system with no serious blood clots?

As far as Miller's "duplicated and modified pre-existing proteins" becoming the regulatory factors is concerned, I could raise the problem of improbability. But beyond that issue, just think about the statement he makes: "The tissues of the body [already] produce a protein known as alpha-1-antitrypsin which binds to the active site of serine proteases found in tissues and keeps them in check." Miller is *presupposing* that a protein that works with the regulated circulatory system we have today, somehow would be present in a primordial organism with low blood pressure. That may be fine to say, but where is the evidence that this is the case for a primordial, low-blood-pressure ancestor to *Homo sapiens*? It seems more reasonable for alpha-1-antitrypsin and antithrombin to both be present to help with the intricacy of the high-powered, super-regulated, blood clotting system humans have today.

If alpha-1-antitrypsin was not present in this hypothetical low pressure system, then Miller's suggestions absolutely break down. Even if this protein was present, I believe natural selection would be more likely to select for a reduction in the complexity of the system rather than advancement of the system to include a protease inhibitor.

There are too many obstacles for the Darwinist to overcome when forming a naturalist, step-by-step explanation of the blood clotting system. (Again, it's not that they don't *have* explanations, it's just that their explanations are not the most logical conclusions based upon the evidence before us.) Therefore, I have found Darwinism to provide unsatisfactory explanations on the origin of blood coagulation. I have simultaneously found Intelligent Design (that the components were designed and placed together at one instance) to provide a much more satisfactory explanation of this phenomenon. There are other things, however, with which ID may not provide a satisfactory explanation. It is in these cases that we must acknowledge the limitations of ID claims, and must acknowledge the possibility of Darwinian evolution as an explanation.

Exceptions to Intelligent Design

The cell membrane is the structure that protects the interior of a cell from the outside environment. It is composed of phospholipids. The "phospho" in the name is due to the phosphate group on the head of the lipid. The lipid has a hydrophilic head (polar), and a hydrophobic tail (nonpolar). Having a polar head and a nonpolar tail causes lipids to form a phospholipid bilayer around the cell. Essentially, the heads of the bilayer face the outside environment and the inside of the cell, while the tails of the bilayer face each other. This happens naturally because of polarity. The tails are attracted to each other because they are nonpolar, and the heads are attracted to the polar liquids on the inside and outside of the cell's membrane.

When lipids are in water, they will line up to form this exact structure on their own. It's similar to how detergents will form bubbles on their own when mixed with water. Regardless of whether or not they are surrounding a cell, they still form this structure and it naturally occurs. So trying to explain the structure of the cell membrane by Intelligent Design is weak because this structure naturally arises almost anywhere you put the lipids. However, when we are discussing machines, or cascades, that are extremely intricate, coded for in the DNA, and irreducibly complex, we have better grounds by which to consider Intelligent Design as an explanation.

Michael Behe (2006) says that, "It is difficult to infer intelligent design from cell membranes" (p. 206).[11] I would agree with Behe in part because lipids form this same structure in the environment naturally. The structures in the cell could have easily evolved to work with this naturally occurring structure. However, I would add that we cannot eliminate design as an explanation in the case of cell membranes. There are many things created that work with something that may not be a part of the initial structure. For instance, dishwashers are created to contain a little compartment for dish soap; however, the dishwasher does not make its own detergent. This means that the structure of the dishwasher was made with the forethought that it would work with something else not made at the same manufacturing plant. The cell could just have easily been designed with the forethought that it would work in conjunction with something that naturally occurs somewhere in the environment. I think the evidence for this explanation is that there are intermembrane proteins coded for in the DNA of the cell. If an intelligent designer made the DNA, then it seems like it made plans for these proteins to be working in conjunction with a cell membrane. The whole point, however, with cell membranes is that you cannot conclude design from their existence. But I think it is also important to note that you cannot exclude design from their existence either.

Discussion

At the start of my freshman year of college, I was very nervous about the science classes I was going to take. I was especially nervous about what I would be learning in my biology classes. I could have been easily swayed into believing in molecules-to-man evolution if the case was convincing enough. However, I was very surprised to see that evolution was not necessary in order to understand any of the life systems that we learned about. In fact, it seemed like the evidence pointed in the opposite direction—towards design. Evolution seemed to just be an anecdotal conclusion thrown in at the end of a discussion about something that appeared to be designed. (Though, I am fairly certain that if I would have taken an evolutionary biology course, a thorough case would have been presented.)

About midway through my first semester—when I was taking an introductory biology course—we were discussing the circulatory system in humans. While my professor was lecturing on the structure and function of the heart, he got his words mixed up. He was saying, as he drew the different chambers of the heart on the board, "As you can see, the *design* of the heart..." He immediately stopped himself and provided a correction to his word choice, "I mean the *structure* of the heart . . . of course, the heart wasn't designed." He then awkwardly proceeded with explaining the intricate ability of the heart to pump blood perfectly through our circulatory system to bring oxygen to the needed areas, and to bring carbon dioxide back to the lungs for emission.

He seemed embarrassed that he had accidentally said design while talking about something in biology—I guess this word is blasphemy in science departments. It was almost as if he couldn't help but use the word *design* because the circulatory system is best described by it.

Of course, this story doesn't prove Intelligent Design—or anything really—other than that it is an example of our minds choosing the most *appropriate* word to describe the appearance of the mechanisms before us. Richard Dawkins even conceded to this point when he wrote the following: "Biology is the study of complicated things that give the appearance of having been designed for a purpose."[37] So Dawkins admits this obvious appearance of design; however, we must remember that looks can be deceiving. We shouldn't let the mere appearance of design lead us to conclude design—which ID enthusiasts are often caught doing—but it is through a thorough investigation of the evidence that leads us to draw the conclusion of Intelligent Design. It is when we study the mechanisms to see if they may be irreducibly complex, and when we look at the odds, that we can be more or less confident in concluding design.

Furthermore, as far as irreducible complexity is concerned, it should be brought to your attention that it cannot be debunked very easily. You see, even if you are able to logically explain how the flagellum came about by natural processes, you still have not explained how all of the *other* irreducibly complex systems in nature have come about by natural processes (such as blood coagulation, cilium, eye, aspects of the immune system, and those that have not yet been formally evaluated). The responsibility is on us to determine which theory best supports these systems' existence: Intelligent Design or Darwinism.

Additionally, when we find a structure that is best explained by Intelligent Design, we should follow the evidence where it leads. We may not like where the evidence is pointing, but then again, what we *like* is irrelevant to the truth.

The two examples of design I have discussed in this chapter

(the bacterial flagellum and blood coagulation) support what is called the *teleological argument*. Essentially, this argument postulates that there is a purpose for the things found in nature because an intelligent source designed them. There is a purpose for the bacterial flagellum: mobility. There is a purpose for blood coagulation: survival. And if the very little things in nature clearly were created for a purpose, things that we need a microscope to see, then perhaps the bigger and more complicated things have bigger purposes.

If we were to pick one thing in nature that may have the biggest overall purpose, it would obviously be the human race. We are clearly the pinnacle of all creation. We are superior to the rest of nature in intellect, creativity, love and sacrifice. From a teleological standpoint, it is reasonable to conclude that our purpose is higher than the animals around us. Perhaps so much higher that it is not even on a physical scale.

You can imagine that all of creation is categorized into a pyramid, with perhaps bacteria at the bottom and humans at the very top. Like all pyramids, the point at the top points straight up to the heavens. Our purpose, being at the top of this pyramid of creation, points to something beyond the physical creation—something *metaphysical*—that may have a link to the very Source of our creation.

Thankfully, there is a very good book on the subject of our purpose that I would encourage you to read. This book is by far the bestselling book of all time. And I think it is because it tells us our purpose. We all see our environment and we cannot ignore the fact of surmounting purpose found there (even when we try to ignore it, it still rises to the surface of our brains), and we are then led to look beyond just nature to discover our ultimate purpose. That is why we turn to the Bible, it provides us with an answer to the most important question we will ever ask: "Why are we here?"

Daniel Faucett

14

THE COSMOS

Throughout time man has sought to answer the question we ended our last discussion with, which was "Why are we here?" Many have rightfully looked to the cosmos. Tracking back into ancient civilizations, we find night sky research from the Babylonians, Egyptians, and Greeks. Their natural human curiosity propelled them into deep studies about outer space— just as recent human curiosity and innovation has landed us on the Moon. According to NASA (2004):

In the third century B.C., Aristarchus of Samos asked the question 'How far away is the Moon?' Incredibly, he was actually able to measure the distance by looking at the shadow of the Earth on the Moon during a lunar eclipse.[12] Other ancient scientists have made notable achievements in figuring distances between observed planets in our solar system by watching signs and shadows in the night sky. (It's really incredible how creative these people were back in the day.) Nevertheless, these advancements throughout human history eventually lead to the discovery that our solar system is insanely massive. But just *how* massive?

According to NASA (2004), "Our Sun, the nearest star, is 93 million miles away;" if you looked at size alone, you would discover that the Sun is "a million times the size of the Earth."[12] The reason our Sun looks so small in the sky is obviously because it is so far away from us. To put this distance into perspective, it would take you seven months to reach the Sun if you travelled in the NASA Space Shuttle (NASA, 2004).[12] Try to imagine travelling in a space ship for seven months. The cool factor would wear off around month two, and then it would be the most boring ride of your life.

However, if we take a step back from our solar system and look at our galaxy, we discover that our solar system is just one small piece of the Milky Way galaxy. The Sun is one of an estimated two-to-four hundred billion stars in our galaxy alone. One can't help but wonder what the planets that orbit those stars must be like—containing their own incredible characteristics, and perhaps even their own lifeforms.

The Milky Way galaxy, however, is so large that travelling at the speed of light would take 100,000 years to travel across its diameter (NASA, 2004).[12] So if there are other planets out there that harbor life, it doesn't seem like we'll be discovering them any time soon. Nevertheless, if you could travel across our galaxy, during your journey you would pass two-to-four hundred billion stars and 100 billion planets. It's no wonder that the comparison between the stars of heaven and the sand upon the seashore is made in the Bible (Genesis 22:17). This comparison may be more accurate than we think, especially if we consider all the suns in the universe, and the possibility of other stars in other galaxies that have not yet been discovered.

It's apparent that our galaxy is huge. But what is beyond our galaxy?

Beyond our galaxy lies an expanse of even more galaxies. The deeper we explore, the more we discover. More and more lights that seem to never end. Gaseous planets, mineral planets, Earth-like planets, dying stars, black holes, asteroid fields, free-floating oxygen, debris, and planets that may have compositions of materials and elements that have never been discovered. There are probably billions of galaxies, maybe even trillions. No one knows for sure how big the universe is, but some estimate that the universe is around 156 billion light years in diameter—which is also always growing due to its expanding nature.[13]

But if God supposedly made all of this, our galaxy and ultimately the universe, then what evidence is there to suggest such a claim?

Evidence of Design in the Universe

If we look at two of the building blocks of atoms, electrons and protons, we find a unique relationship that points in the direction of Intelligent Design. The ratio of electron to proton mass is 1:1836.15267389—meaning that it requires about 1836 electrons to equal the mass of one proton.[14] This ratio is vital to the ability of our universe to even have molecules. If it were not for this 1:1836 mass ratio between electrons and protons, molecules would not have formed in the universe because the ability of atoms and molecules to form depends on relative mass and relative charge of the constituents. If this ratio were different, we would not have molecules and we definitely would not have life in the universe. But miraculously, we have molecules because we have this finely-tuned ratio between electron and proton mass. Because of this amazing fact, every atom, molecule, and compound is able to exist.

However, looking beyond the small things we find just as much evidence of design and fine tuning with our massive solar system as we do with the little system that is an atom. In our solar system, we find that the Earth is an optimal distance away from the Sun for the water cycle to exist. If the Earth were too close to the Sun, the water on the Earth would boil constantly and thus lifeforms depending on liquid water could not survive. If the Earth were too far away from the Sun we would have the opposite problem, all the water would be stone-hard ice. So the distance the Earth is from the Sun is vital to the survival of lifeforms on planet Earth, and it seems as though we have been placed in the perfect spot.

It is not only the location of the Earth that is significant. The 23-degree axial tilt of the Earth is vital to the ability of Earth to harbor life. Too much one way or the other and our planet would be either too cold, or too hot, for life to exist.

The oxygen levels are in a happy medium that keeps fires from spontaneously erupting on the Earth's surface. The carbon dioxide levels are also maintained at the right level. Too much carbon dioxide, and the greenhouse effect would cause ridiculously high temperatures; too little, and the plants that cover our planet wouldn't be able to perform photosynthesis. Without photosynthesis—the process that takes in carbon dioxide and produces oxygen—none of us would be here. We have to have oxygen to survive, and it needs to be maintained within a precise range.

The features of the Earth and the electron-to-proton mass ratio are examples of *anthropic constants*. Essentially, an anthropic constant is any precise, interdependent, and finely-tuned environmental factor in the universe that allows life to exist. (Anthropic is translated from a Greek word that means human.) These constants are derived from observations of the universe, and collectively support what is known as the "Anthropic Principle." The Anthropic Principle postulates that the universe is precisely designed to allow life on Earth to exist.

Another anthropic constant in the universe is our Moon. It plays a very important role in the survival of lifeforms on Earth.

From the discovery of gravity by Issac Newton, we know that objects are attracted to each other based on their masses and the distance between them. Consequently, the Moon inflicts a force on the Earth, and the Earth inflicts a force on the Moon. This force is responsible for keeping the Moon in a slightly receding orbit, and for causing the high and low tides on Earth.

The central idea behind the origin of the Moon is that around 4.5 billion years ago, the Earth was hit by a "Mars-size planetary embryo" into its initial first rotation of roughly twelve hours per day (Dorminey, 2009).[15] Shortly after this collision, molten mantle was thrown back into orbit and thus amalgamated into the Moon we have today (Dorminey, 2009).[15] This is known as *The Giant Impactor Theory*.

The Moon, whether you believe it was created by God, or the product of a collision with the Earth, is important because it provides reciprocal gravitational force on the Earth due to its unusually large size. According to Lisle (2013), "Earth's moon is the fifth-largest moon in [our] solar system. It is over one quarter the size of Earth in diameter. No other planet has a moon this large in proportion to the size of the planet."[16] This gravitational pull is important because it provides Earth with tides that clean our ocean shores. This pull is also important because it slows down the Earth's rotation, allowing the Earth to stay warm. If we did not have the Moon, every day would be shorter, temperatures would be too cold for plants to grow, and life on Earth would be an impossibility.

The size of Jupiter is also an anthropic constant. Jupiter has a diameter 11.2 times greater than the Earth; this massive size allows Jupiter to have a very strong gravitational pull on various objects that come through our solar system. There are many comets that have avoided Earth because of this fact; Jupiter has simply pulled them into herself before they have the opportunity to crash into Earth. In essence, Jupiter is our cosmic protector. Or, perhaps our cosmic vacuum, sucking into herself comets and asteroids before they reach the inner solar system.

In 1993, the massive Comet Shoemaker-Levy 9 was discovered as it orbited Jupiter. Fortunately for humans, in 1994, Jupiter took on the impact as the comet broke into twenty-one separate fragments that crashed into the planet's surface. This comet would have dealt a deathly blow to Earth if Jupiter had not been there to protect us.

It's important to note, though, that while our solar system is finely tuned, so too is our galaxy. You see, our solar system orbits extremely far from the center of the Milky Way. It lies between what is known as the spiral arms. This location provides our planet with one of the most unique and favorable positions in the galaxy. Fortunately for us, our Sun lies within the galactic co-rotation radius (Mishurov & Zenina, 1999).[17] This gives us a unique solar stability because the stars in our galaxy orbit the center of the galaxy at a different rate than the trailing spiral arms. Therefore, most stars that are located between the spiral arms do not stay there permanently, but eventually are swept inside a spiral arm.[18] Only at a precise distance from the galaxy's center, the "co-rotation radius," can a star remain in its place between two spiral arms, orbiting at precisely the same rate as the galaxy arms rotate around the core (Deem, 2008).[18] Our Sun is near the co-rotation resonance where the rotation velocities of the disk and the spiral pattern match (Mishurov & Zenina, 1999).[17]

If we happened to be located in the spiral arms, our ability to see the galaxy would be seriously impaired because of space debris (Deem, 2008).[18] Also, if we were in a more densely occupied area, then planetary orbits could be disrupted, and all life on Earth could be destroyed (Deem, 2008).[18]

Even beyond our galaxy we find tremendous evidence of design. However, to explain this you must first understand that our universe is expanding.

Observations of distant stars have revealed a *redshift*. (A redshift is simply an effect that happens to the wavelength of light when the object giving off light moves away from the observer; the reverse of this is a *blueshift*, which is the exact opposite scenario that occurs when the object moves toward the observer.) Additionally, radiation afterglow was discovered—which is radiation that must have been given off by an explosion in the distant past (that we now call the Big Bang). Through these two discoveries, we can conclude that the universe had a beginning, and that the universe is expanding.[36]

Due to the arrival and support of the Big Bang theory, scientists soon proposed that there should be ripples in the temperature leftover from the Big Bang's cosmic radiation. If these ripples did exist, then scientists would be able to provide an explanation for the accumulation of matter that allowed our galaxies to form. In 1989, NASA's famous COBE (Cosmic Background Explorer) was sent out to find an answer to this fascinating prediction. By 1992, with its sophisticated equipment, COBE was able to determine that these ripples did in fact exist! And not only did they exist, but they were incredibly precise. According to Geisler and Turek (2004):

The ripples [showed] that the explosion and expansion of the universe was precisely tweaked to cause just enough matter to congregate to allow galaxy formation, but not enough to cause the universe to collapse back on itself. Any slight variation one way or the other, and none of us would be here to tell about it. (p. 83)[32]

These ripples are so ideal that they are considered to be precise down to one part in one hundred thousand (that's 1 to 100,000).[32] George Smoot, NASA's project leader for the COBE mission, said that these ripples were "the fingerprints of the maker."[33,36]

Nevertheless, we find ourselves placed in a universe with design at every level. Whether we look at protons or the universe as a whole, we can't seem to escape the residue of an intelligent designer. We miraculously have clustered matter that perfectly established our galaxy. We are located in a supreme position in the solar system that gives us the perfect conditions for life. Our solar system is placed within our galaxy in such a way that we are safe from harm's way. And our Earth is placed in such a spot of the galaxy that we are able to see the grandeur of the heavens. Could it be the case that all of this is just a coincidence?

Albert Einstein once said, "God does not play dice with the universe."[41,42] I agree with Einstein on this point. But ultimately you must decide that for yourself. For me personally,

I don't have enough faith in materialism to believe that all of this was a coincidence. I think your conclusion about the presence of an intelligent designer will not rest on how much faith you have in God, but on how much faith you are willing to have in materialism.

Multiverse Theory

People will often reply to these arguments posed by intelligent design enthusiasts with the *multiverse theory*. This theory essentially offers a hypothetical set of multiple universes (finite or infinite), and would include the universe that we live in today. Each subsequent universe could be described as an alternate or parallel universe. Our universe may seem to be precisely designed at every level, but that is only because we reside in one of those multiple universes where the odds are in our favor.

Let me make it clear that in order to justify that God did not make our universe, you must believe in multiple universes to explain away the improbable aspects of our own universe that we have already discussed. In reference to the precision of the cosmic temperature ripples, you must at least believe that there are 100,000 universes in order to explain how our universe got the radiation ripples *just* right. And when you combine the other aspects of improbability, such as Earth's distance from the sun and our elemental composition; the odds become even worse for the materialist, and he or she must increase this number of possible universes exponentially.

First off, this theory itself is self-defeating. The definition of universe is that it is all of time and space and matter. To say that there are multiple "all time, space, and matter-including universes" is contradictory and collapses on itself by definition. There must only be one universe that holds everything based on its definition, otherwise, we must change the definition of the word universe.

The multiverse theory is sort of like if I said, "Everything in this room was 100% made in China, *and* everything in this room was 100% made in America." The statements themselves contradict each other. Either it was all made in China, or it was all made in America. Otherwise, I should not have used the terms *everything* or *100%*. The same product cannot be 100% made in two different places, it could, however, be 50% made in one region and 50% made in another. We can use the terms *100%* and *everything*, but it is incorrect to do so. We should either use different terminology or change the definitions of the words we use.

Additionally, I think it is important to note that there is no evidence for other universes. These other universes are completely hypothetical and untestable. The suggestion that they exist is clearly based on the presupposition that God cannot exist. They are supported only by the wishful thinking of materialists. (Which is quite ironic, you would think a materialist would be the last person to suggest a theory that is untestable and analogous to Greek mythology.) According to Sciama (1993), there are obvious objections to the multiverse theory:

1. The hypothesis is much too extravagant and bizarre to be credible.

2. It violates the well established tradition in theoretical physics to explain phenomena deductively from a fundamental theory.

3. The multiverse hypothesis has no real predictive power.

4. It is pointless or unscientific to postulate the existence of other universes, many of which are unobservable even in principle.[34,35]

Science is centered around testability and the predictive power of theories. The multiverse theory is untestable, not possible by definition, and scientifically counterintuitive. Therefore, in order to believe in this theory, you must throw out science altogether. (This is shaky ground for materialists, who often pride themselves in *material* evidence!) The materialist actually has blind faith that there are other universes out there for which there is no evidence. The fact that the multiverse theory even exists shows the bias and *faith* of materialists.

Those who are so quick to accept the multiverse theory

should ask themselves why they are so quick to accept something for which there is no evidence, in comparison to accepting a God for which our entire universe is evidence? They have thrown out a reasonable explanation of the finely-tuned universe for an unreasonable explanation of the finely-tuned universe.

The materialist may reply to this logic by saying, "There may be no evidence for multiple universes, but there's also no evidence for God." The problem with this argument is that it just isn't true. The idea that God made the universe is grounded in factual evidence and observations of the universe. The theistic view is based on an analysis of the *one* universe that there *is* evidence for—rather than being based on the wishful thinking of materialists' hypothetical multiple universes. I think it is vital to understand the difference here. On one side we have a theist pointing towards the evidence; on the other side we have a materialist pointing towards imagination.

Light

When I look at the character of God and His magnificence, and relate that to the massive, complex, finely-tuned and elegantly-designed universe that we *do* have evidence for, I am astounded at the appropriateness. It is so suitable for a magnificent God to have a magnificent creation. His fingerprint is all over the heavens, and the more we discover the more we can be confident in this claim. It seems as though Genesis 1:1 was right all along, "In the beginning God created the heavens and the earth" (NIV). To me, it is so unbelievably obvious that an intelligent designer made the cosmos, yet many people still deny this truth and hold onto a materialist explanation. Why are people so eager to adopt theories like the multiverse, knowing that there is no evidence for such claims?

Materialists often justify their views by attacking the Bible—the most reliable document in support of an intelligent designer. They say that their view is the most appropriate in light of the Bible being "inaccurate." One of their biggest arguments is that the Bible contradicts what we know about light's character and behavior. For example, light was once thought to travel at an infinite speed. It was theorized that there was no delay in its travel time and pathway. There was no reason to believe otherwise until Ole Christensen Romer, a Danish astronomer who invented the modern thermometer, discovered that light had a finite speed by observing around 140 eclipses of Jupiter's moon—known as *Io*— in 1676.

If light has a finite speed, then this seems to contradict the biblical description of light in Genesis 1:3, "And God said, 'Let there be light,' and there was light" (NIV). This suggests an instantaneous (or infinite) character of light; which supposedly contradicts the finite character of light that we now know light exhibits. However, upon further investigation, we find that God—and his creation—is not bound by physical laws.

When we look at God's six-day creation, we notice a lot of physical laws of nature being broken. For example, when God tells the land to produce trees, the trees instantly grow, there is no delay. When God makes man from the dust of the earth, He did not have to wait for Adam to grow up, He made Him as an adult. When Jesus Christ healed the servants ear in the Garden of Gethsemane, it was immediately rejuvenated. Or when Christ commanded the immense storm at the Sea of Galilee to calm, it did. The disciples were so surprised that in Mark 4:41 they said, "Who is this? Even the wind and the waves obey him!" (NIV). My point is this: There is no resistance by the laws of nature when God commands His dominion over them. After all, He did invent the laws of nature.

Likewise, when God created light, He did not have to wait for it to arrive from stars that are billions of lightyears away because light was made mature in form—as Adam was made mature in form. And why would God make all His heavenly creation invisible to humans if the whole purpose of His creation is for *His* glory, and the revelation of *His* existence? It does not make sense for God to wait on all the stars' light to arrive at Earth; that is why He made light already "there" from the beginning—just as Genesis chapter one tells us. It's also why God put us in the exact spot of the galaxy that allows us to see the rest of the universe clearly.

But how did God make light *mature* in form? Jeremiah 10:12 tells us, "by His understanding He has stretched out the heavens." Our observations of the universe indicate that it is expanding at an accelerated rate. This fits the picture of how God could have "stretched out the heavens." Additionally, it explains how light was instantaneously created and stretched to fill the vacuum of space.

This instantaneous creation of light also explains why we can see stars that are billions of lightyears away. We can see these stars, not necessarily because our Earth has been here for billions of years, but because God said, "Let there be light" and there was light; and because God *stretched* out the heavens to make light mature in form. This light could have instantly filled the vacuum of space if it was created *in* the vacuum of space.

Therefore, my conclusion is that the arguments against the biblical description of light are not grounded on an investigation into what the Bible actually says about light, or how God made the universe. The Bible does not contradict the character of light, nor does it contradict scientific observations of the universe. The character of light has not changed since creation, but when God made light, he made it mature in form by stretching out the heavens; just like He made Adam mature in form, Eve, the oceans, the birds of the air, and the fish of the sea.

Discussion

At every turn in the cosmos, one is forced to recognize design. But do the heavens reveal anything about God? After all, He did create them like a painter paints a picture, and every painting contains some trace of the artist, so God's creation should contain some traces of Himself. According to Romans 1:20, "For since the creation of the world God's invisible qualities—his eternal power and divine nature—have been clearly seen, being understood from what has been made, so that people are without excuse" (NIV). So, through observing God's creation, God is revealed.

God's existence, power and divinity are so evident from His creation that we cannot use "science" as an excuse to write God off. We cannot claim that science disproves God because our observations of the universe clearly reinforces the existence of Him (or at least the existence of a wise designer). This fact of design is undeniable based on our observations of the universe. I believe that somewhere, perhaps in the deepest recesses of our souls, we all understand this truth.

Psalm 33:5-6 says, "The Lord loves righteousness and justice; the earth is full of his unfailing love. By the word of the Lord the heavens were made, their starry host by the breath of his mouth" (NIV). Part of God's justice is that He allows His creation to be plainly seen. His creation reveals Himself; therefore, no one is excluded from experiencing, in some form or fashion, God's creation. So, it is a form of justice to be given the evidence before the trial, so to speak.

However, I think people need something more than just observational evidence of the universe in order to find God. It was not my observations of the universe that saved me or convinced me of God; it was the invasion of the Holy Spirit into my heart. My observations of the universe simply point back to that which is now in me. In fact, most of what I know about science came long after I had already developed a relationship with Jesus.

People will often say, though, that they need more than observations of the painting. They want to see the artist in order to believe. For instance, I've often heard people say, "If God wants us to acknowledge Him, then why doesn't God show Himself to us in person?"

The reason God doesn't reveal Himself to you in person is because it wouldn't help you to believe in Him. I say this with confidence because of how the Jewish people treated Jesus Christ. Jesus performed miracles of healing, salvation, raising of the dead (and from the dead), turning water into wine, and the forgiveness of sins. He fulfilled the biblical prophecies that the coming Messiah was supposed to fulfill on His first visit.

However, the Jews still rejected and crucified Him. So if Jesus, who is Himself God, was seen by the Jews face-to-face and was still rejected, what makes you think that you would behave any differently if you saw Jesus face-to-face today?

According to these truths, we can rest assured that seeing isn't always believing. This should be even more obvious to us now that we have so much overwhelming evidence of design that has been discovered on Earth, and especially in the universe abroad.

To further my point, Luke 16:31 tells us that if you do not listen to Moses and the prophets, then you will not be convinced about God even if someone rises from the dead—which Jesus did Himself. On several occasions the Jewish priests would ask Jesus to demonstrate His authority by giving them a sign. But Jesus did no such thing because their hearts were hardened. Today, I believe we are just like the Jews. We need spiritual revelation from God, not a physical sign to be able to believe. The physical signs are all around us in the form of His creation, yet we still do not believe. We would rather choose to believe that our location in the universe—that which is incredibly tuned for safety, life sustainability, and visibility of the surrounding astronomical bodies—is simply coincidental.

We don't see it because we don't *want* to see it. The result is that our hearts are hardened, and we lose track of why we were put here in the first place. You see, it is inherent in all of us to ask the question, "Why are we here?" But in order to answer this question accurately, we must answer a similar question: "Why did God make us?"

The Bible tells us that God made us, as well as all things, for His glory. So there seems to be a common denominator between all matter: It points back to its Creator. Psalm 19:1 says, "The heavens declare the glory of God; the skies proclaim the work of his hands" (NIV). Everything is basically the product of His hands for the purpose of his glory. Why else would God place us in a particular place in the galaxy where we can see the rest of the universe? He placed us in the exact spot where we would be able to safely see the works of His hands. He made light mature in form so that we would be able to see the starry host of the cosmos and glorify Him for it.

There is a reason that isolated people groups from all over the world since the beginning of time have worshipped and served a god in some shape or form. There is a reason that there is something inherent in us that leads us to acknowledge a creator. I believe God placed an inherent knowledge of Him in all our brains because we are made in the image of Him. Having been made in the image of Him gives us certain characteristics. I believe that an acknowledgement of a higher power—of a creator for the creation—is one of those inherent qualities we possess, having been made in the image of God. It is in the internal wiring of our brains. That is why it takes a lifetime of indoctrination, interpretations of evidence (which the interpretations are not hard facts), and debate to convince a fellow that He wasn't created.

But speaking of evidence, with so many planets out there in the universe, and "infinite" time, it stands to reason that life should exist out there somewhere other than Earth. According to some U.S. researchers, there are many Earth-like planets in the universe.[19] These planets supposedly contain deep oceans that could harbor life, and may be present in as many as one third of solar systems outside of Earth's.[19] However, according to opponents of this proposition, these Earth-like planets haven't been proven to exist, they are merely speculations generated from computer simulations of various types of solar systems forming.[20]

So whether these Earth-like planets exist is just speculation. To date, we have not discovered any spec of life on any other planet we have observed. Our Mars rovers roam the red planet in search of any signs of life as they hopelessly find absolutely nothing. Is this merely a coincidence that there is no life outside of Earth, or is there something special and unique about Earth? Perhaps God made Earth, with synchronized orbits, the cosmos, and a prime location in the universe to reveal His hand in creation.

Whether you believe in God or not, you must acknowledge the miracle of our existence in the universe. Our placement in the galaxy; our stability that supports life; our healthy temperature; our Moon's size; the inherent wiring of our brains that logically chooses to acknowledge a creator; the fact that there is no life on other planets (as far as we know), and the fingerprint of His hand in every created thing. Whether everything is a miracle of Intelligent Design, or random explosions and planetary collisions, we are all still the product of a miracle. And I believe the miracle of our existence simply points to the reason we are here.

In order to discover the reason we are here, we should follow where the universe is pointing. I believe it's quite obviously pointing towards a designer. So, perhaps we should ask the Designer Himself why we are here.

If we found an oddly shaped clay pot, the best way to discover its purpose would be to ask its designer. We could try all day to figure out its purpose on our own, and we probably would get very close to determining it. But, ultimately, we could never be 100% sure of its purpose until the designer told us. Similarly, the best way to discover our purpose is to ask the One who designed us. However, just as a clay pot is different than man in its composition, so is God different in His composition. The God who made this universe is probably not even composed of materials when in His natural scene. I would expect Him to be manifest in a different dimension altogether (especially when you consider His superiority to us being infinitely large). Therefore, I believe we must look beyond our universe—our current dimension—and we must ask the Designer why we are here.

The Bible is a book that talks about this other dimension. It makes a lot of claims about the spiritual world by discussing sin, angels, God, Satan, demons, our inherent condition, and the purpose of our lives. Some of the statements we may not like, such as the ones about hell, but if they are true then how we feel about them is irrelevant. However, the concern we all have is this: Can we trust what the Bible says about the spiritual dimension? In our next meeting, I will discuss why the Bible is reliable, and why we can trust what it tells us about our purpose—something that extends well beyond our material existence.

15

THE RELIABILITY OF THE BIBLE

Let's define reliable: "Suitable or fit to be relied on" (dependable), "giving the same result on successive trials."[21] Many of the numbers found from carbon dating are thrown out because we now realize that the production of carbon-14 has changed through time (the radiation from the Sun has fluctuated).[22] So, it seems that carbon dating is not fully reliable because of this phenomenon—based on the Merriam-Webster definition of the word because it has not given the same result on successive trials. If we held the Bible to this standard, how would it compare? Does it change over time? How reliable is it, and how do we test its reliability?

To test the reliability of the Bible, we should analyze different manuscripts and copies to see if they give us the same result; we should analyze the texts themselves to look for contradictions; we should look at anthropological discoveries, and we should look at its historical reliability when compared to secular texts. First, let us look at the different manuscripts.

Are the different manuscripts of the Bible consistent with each other? In other words, do we have reliability here? We have more than 24,000 manuscript copies of the New Testament (Keathley, 2004).[23] There is no other document of ancient times containing this amount of attestable data—the Iliad by Homer only contains 643 surviving manuscripts.[23] Some papyri fragments of the New Testament texts range anywhere from 135 A.D. to the eighth century (Keathley, 2004).[23] So we know we have the sample data, it surpasses the closest document by a factor of more than thirty-seven, and it ranges over a very large time period. So, let's look to see if there are any contradictions in these different manuscripts.

With 5,686 Greek manuscripts that can be cross-checked, the consistency of the copies of the New Testament can be determined. This process of cross-checking these documents has determined the consistency of the New Testament documents to be about 99.5% (Slick, 2008).[24] (The 24,000-manuscript number comes by taking a total sum of the over 19,000 translations of the New Testament—which consisted of

242

Syriac, Latin, Coptic, and Aramaic languages). 99.5% consistency.

How can a document as old as time be so consistent, having passed through so many hands? I believe it's because the hand of God has been with it. It's really a modern miracle. After all, Jesus did say in Mathew 24:35, "Heaven and earth will pass away, but my words will not pass away." I have long thought that this verse was only a spiritual statement, but I have now found it to be applicable to both the spiritual realm as well as our earthly experience with God's Word.

However, with all these manuscripts, shouldn't there be major doctrinal contradictions between them? We would expect upon further study that we would find contradictions; however, what we find is quite on the contrary, what we find is staggering consistency. As a result of this, critics must resort to finding contradiction within the Bible itself (such as within a major translation of the text), rather than trying to find contradiction within the different manuscripts. And they would be right to pursue this level of skepticism. After all, I take the same level of skepticism against other religions; it is only fair that we take an unabridged and skeptical look at Christianity. Therefore, as Reading Rainbow would say, "Take a look, it's in a book." The answers to our skepticisms towards the Bible can be found through an honest and thorough investigation *of* the Bible—the book that Christians claim to be the very words of the Creator. And this great book is either a fact of truth, or a lie perpetuated by fiction. It is nothing in-between.

Are There Contradictions in the Christian Bible?

There are passages in the Bible that, at the first time reading them, you would think they contradicted other passages in scripture. However, upon further study, you will find that there are zero contradictions in the entire Bible. I know that statement may seem like an outrageous claim to you, and it should. It must seem insane for someone to claim that a book that big and old has no contradictions, but it's simply the objective reality we have discovered. To demonstrate this claim, I will address some of the supposed contradictions I have heard from skeptics. But first, let us establish the richness of the Bible.

The Bible consists of sixty-six books ranging from a variety of forty different authors.[25] These forty different authors had a vast array of life experiences, and lived through various time periods in history. Some of these authors were shepherds, farmers, physicians, fisherman (such as some of the disciples), priests, prophets, philosophers, and even kings.[25] The Bible was written over a period of 1,500 years in three languages (Hebrew, Aramaic, and Greek); dating back to nearly 1,500 B.C. [25] The Bible was the first book ever printed, and was done so in 1454 A.D. by Johannes Gutenberg.[25] So, even if you don't believe the Bible is true and without fault, you must respect the richness and historical importance of this incredible document. A document that has transported time and impacted civilization after civilization. A book this rich deserves a closer look at the skeptics claims about supposed contradictions.

For biblical contradiction number one, let's look at the number one contradiction on the "101 Contradictions in the Bible" list found on the Answering Christianity website. This supposed contradiction essentially states: In 2nd Samuel 24:1, the Bible says God incited David to count the fighting men of Israel; but, in 1st Chronicles 21:1, it says Satan did. So, who really incited David to count the fighting men of Israel?[26] It can't be both God and Satan; therefore, the conclusion is that this is a biblical contradiction. Let's check it out for ourselves.

Second Samuel 24:1 says, "Now again the anger of the Lord burned against Israel, and it incited David against them to say, 'Go, number Israel and Judah.'" (NASB). Now, the important thing to note here is that God doesn't move King David to sin. It just shows us that as a result of God's anger towards David, that this anger incited David to fall into sin. God didn't make David sin, nor did God tempt David. The question is though, who directly tempted David to sin and number the people? The answer is in 1st Chronicles 21:1; which says, "Then Satan stood up against Israel and moved David to number Israel" (NASB). So clearly God did not tempt David, but he allowed—or worded more appropriately, *suffered*—David to be moved by the Devil.

This is another claim that can be debunked through about ten minutes of research and reading the biblical text. Yet, it is small claims like this that lead people away from the Bible. Please do not throw away God and the Bible because of surface-level, out-of-context proposed contradictions that are not true. In these verses particularly, they even complement each other and tell you the full picture of what happened! God's anger towards David simply opened up an opportunity for Satan to move him in a rebellious direction.

Supposed biblical contradiction number two: the idea that Genesis chapter one and Genesis chapter two contradict each other. I've heard much debate about this supposed contradiction, so I looked into it and found that this contradiction is based off the sequencing of the chapters.

Chapter one describes the creation of plants, followed by the creation of animals, and then humans. Whereas chapter two seems to describe the creation of humans first, followed by the creation of plants, and then animals (Deem, 2009).[27] Sequence is important. You'll notice I reference the same argument from Michael Behe to discredit the hypothesis that a bacterial flagellum could have evolved in a step-by-step,

Darwinian fashion (especially when I reference the problem of the T3SS as an evolutionary explanation). Therefore, it is only fair that we look at the biblical sequence skeptically as well.

Genesis 1:1 through 2:3 provides us with a sequential account of what God made on each of the six days during the creation week. Whereas Genesis 2:4 through verse twenty-five focuses specifically on day six (Chaffey, 2010).[28] Basically, on day six, according to Genesis two, the order of events are as follows: Adam is created, Garden of Eden is created, Adam is put in the Garden and given instructions, Adam names some of the kinds of animals, God creates Eve, and we are given a depiction of the first marriage (Chaffey, 2010).[28] The issue is that people believe the chronological order of created man, animals, and trees is in contradiction with Genesis one. This is not the case.

Genesis 2:7 says, "Then the Lord God formed man of dust from the ground, and breathed into his nostrils the breath of life; and man became a living being" (NASB). After the creation of man, Genesis 2:9 tells us, "Out of the ground the LORD God caused to grow every tree that is pleasing to the sight and good for food; the tree of life also in the midst of the garden, and the tree of the knowledge of good and evil" (NASB). Then, in Genesis 2:19, the Bible mentions what seems to be the present-tense creation of certain animals, "the Lord God formed every beast of the field and every bird of the sky" (NASB). Take note of the translation quoted here.

At first read, of course this seems to be a contradiction because Genesis one lays out that the animals and trees were created before man, and Genesis two seems to say otherwise. However, when we look at the original language we can resolve this supposed contradiction quite easily. The Hebrew word for formed in both passages is *yatsar*.[28] According to Answers in Genesis writer Tim Chaffey (2016):

> The New King James Version . . . translates the verb in its perfect form. However, this Hebrew word may also be translated in its pluperfect form. In this case, it would read that God "had formed" these creatures, as some other translations have it translated (e.g. ESV, NIV, etc.).[28]

So when we look at Genesis 2:19 when translated in its pluperfect form, it would be more appropriately read as, "Now the Lord God *had formed* out of the ground all the beasts of the field and all the birds of the air" (NIV).

This translation, since it reads "had formed," creates zero contradiction in the chronological order of creation between Genesis chapter one and Genesis chapter two. Because this means that God had (past-tense) formed the beasts of the field. Which God had already done earlier in the creation week as outlined in Genesis chapter one.

We cannot look at specific translations that deviate from the original manuscripts and then assume that those contradictions found are true for the originals also. This is skewed logic when analyzing any document, not just the Bible. This supposed contradiction is resolved as well as the first. However, this contradiction needed to be resolved by further study into the original Hebrew in the original manuscripts. On the one hand, critics were right to say that there was a contradiction; but on the other hand, their claims are based on a misunderstanding of the original language. So, what is our conclusion concerning this contradiction? The critics must accept that this supposed contradiction is unsupported. The Bible is still accurate. The original manuscripts are as true today as they were thousands of years ago when they were written.

Supposed biblical contradiction number three—or really a supposed biblical error—is the question as to why Jesus was baptized by John the Baptist. In Mathew 3:11 the Bible says that John baptized for repentance, but if Jesus was without sin, why would He need to repent? This is often considered one of the big "Jesus errors" because it apparently shows a contradiction between who Jesus says He is, and what Jesus did on Earth to back up the claims. However, upon further investigation into who Jesus really was (and is), and why he came, it becomes pretty clear as to why Jesus got baptized.

For one, just because Jesus got baptized doesn't mean that Jesus considered Himself a sinner, or that Jesus was a sinner. There is no record of Him sinning in the Bible, so why should we assume that the Bible is telling us that Jesus needed to repent? He has no reason to repent. However, in Mathew 3:14–15, Jesus comes to John for baptism:

> And John tried to prevent Him, saying, "I need to be baptized by You, and are You coming to me?" But Jesus answered and said to him, "Permit it to be so now, for thus it is fitting for us to fulfill all righteousness." Then he allowed Him. (NKJV)

It is extremely important to note what Jesus did *not* say. Jesus did not say that it is fitting for Him to be baptized so He could *attain* righteousness. What He actually said is that it is fitting for Him to be baptized to *fulfill* righteousness. There is a misconception here that Jesus is implying righteousness attained; but in reality it is on the contrary, He is saying righteousness fulfilled, and there is obviously a massive theological difference.

Additionally, there is a parallel here to Jesus' statement in Matthew 5:17, "Do not think that I came to abolish the Law or the Prophets; I did not come to abolish but to fulfill"[29] (NASB). So, perhaps this was an example of Jesus fulfilling one of the righteous requirements to be Israel's Messiah.

Another reason Christ may have been baptized is to show an example of the Trinity. If you remember, this is when the Holy Spirit descended as a dove, and the voice of God the Father said, "This is My beloved Son, with whom I am well pleased" (ESV). A perfect picture of the Trinity—the Triune God displayed in the Son (Jesus), the Holy Spirit (the dove), and the Father (the voice). As well as a direct example of God the Father showing his approval towards His Son; thus attesting to the authenticity of Jesus.

Essentially, there are many ways to interpret the event of Jesus' baptism. However, none of the logical ways to view this event can result in the conclusion of Biblical inaccuracy. Furthermore, it is wrong to assume Jesus was seeking repentance—or needing repentance. A lot of what Jesus did, and said, is above my head and my understanding, but just because Jesus said something that's hard to understand doesn't make it wrong or contradictory. With the Bible, like all things superbly intelligent, it requires intense investigation to understand. I've seen so many people doubt it simply because they don't understand it. I'm just as guilty as the next person, I have doubted Jesus and the Bible many times because I haven't understood them. However, every time I have looked into the Word deeper it has always been proven true. The problem comes when we refuse to put in the hard mental work that is required to understand something so immensely superior to ourselves (and even then we can come up short).

I think it is also hard to understand the Bible because it is so deep, similar to an ocean. When we try to investigate it, we can quite easily get lost in the waves. (In this case, waves composed of worldly doubt and confusion that try to keep us from diving deeper.) However, when we dedicate our time, minds, and hearts, we can get through the waves and experience depths of unmatched understanding and peace. While we will never understand everything there is to know about God's Word, we can at least learn enough to discover our purpose.

I think for everyone who comes to know the Lord, there is an experience of breaking through the waves and discovering their purpose. That moment when they quit letting the world tell them how to view the Bible and they start letting their hearts and minds unleash on its fruit. It is in these moments especially that they experience the most understanding.

When it comes to science, we don't give up on it when our observations are puzzling. We also don't give up on it when our theories are wrong. We move on, throw away useless theories and adopt new ones that match objective reality better. When things are puzzling, we simply attempt to put the pieces together and learn as much as possible. I believe that this is what we should do with the biblical text. When things are puzzling and hard to understand, we should dive deeper into study. We should develop theories and hold them up to the test of God's full Word. We should not write the Word itself off as contradictory simply because of a surface-level reading—or because of inadequate theories of God's nature and existence. Of course, if at the end of a true and genuine study of the Word we find it to be false, then we should abandon it. For me and countless others, though, the more we learn about the Bible the more our faith is strengthened in its reliability. The more we learn about supposed contradictions and their weak foundations, the more we believe that the Bible doesn't have any contradictions at all.

Daniel Faucett

16

THE SPIRITUAL TAXONOMY OF DOUBT

My life has been mingled with doubt. Throughout different stages it seems that there has been a particular doubt that I have struggled with the most. During the beginning years of my life, I had an inherent belief in God because of the home that I grew up in (which I am extremely grateful for). However, growing up through middle and high school I started to really struggle with the doubt that God even existed. After all, there is so much "evidence" that says the Bible is historically and scientifically inaccurate, right? We've all heard teachers, scientists and professors say that we are nothing more than evolved animals. I used to struggle with these ideas and views.

I believe the Devil uses these ideas and views to create doubt. And this doubt keeps us from growing closer to the Lord. He wants you to think that God doesn't exist because Satan doesn't want you to pursue the One who can give you freedom, peace, purpose, and salvation.

However, after I started to develop a relationship with Jesus, these doubts became less and less prominent in my mind. They slowly became a less effective attack on my spiritual life. All it took was looking at both sides of the argument.

If all you do is listen to modern research on the age of fossils, then you are going to start doubting the claim of a young Earth—that seems to be outlined in the Bible. However, if you look into the theoretical basis of radiometric dating, you start to realize that the estimate ages are not set-in-stone, cold-hard facts. They are theoretically based, and as a result, cannot prove anything. I also considered that even if the Earth is billions of years old, that still doesn't mean God doesn't exist or that the Bible is inaccurate. There are irreducibly complex biological machines and cascades that must have been designed—otherwise, they would not exist. Also, when looking at God and time, there is great evidence that prophecy in the Bible has been miraculously fulfilled.

But regardless of looking at both sides of things, you have to develop a relationship with Jesus Christ in order to really get rid of doubt. It is the result of my relationship with Him that has protected me from the flaming arrows of the Evil One— not just researching deeper into scientific claims. While the research helps us understand why we believe, as well as strengthening our faith, it's our relationship with Jesus that is our *source* of faith.

Needless to say, the doubts are there for all of us, and I believe we can diagram these doubts in what I call The Spiritual Taxonomy of Doubt.

FIGURE 16.1

THE SPIRITUAL TAXONOMY OF DOUBT

What's interesting about the diagram (Figure 16.1), though, is that at the top there is not another doubt. Usually, as pictured in Bloom's Taxonomy—which addresses the hierarchy of learning—the arrangement is much more consistent. For example, the top of this diagram should have the most severe or least severe doubt. However, this taxonomy is slightly different. It's more of a journey, and it goes in decreasing order of doubt strength until we reach the pinnacle of our life experience.

At the bottom of this triangle we have the ultimate doubt. The doubt that the Devil really wants to keep us in for as long as possible: Does God Exist? I mean, after all, there is so much surmounting "evidence" that proves that matter came from nothing without a first cause, and that the idea of God making everything is an impossibility. We must have evolved; therefore, we were not created—or, at least, this is the reasoning that persists among our world that is simply based on the presupposition that God cannot exist..

If Satan can keep us here, he's won. However, I believe most people usually make it out of this stage. Eventually, after divine revelation, and after one observes the environment that God has made; one usually comes to the realization that the amazing order, complexity, and magnificence of the Earth, solar system, and universe is so incredible that a higher being must have made it. After all, around 89% of Americans believe in "God or a universal spirit" for a reason.[30] There is something undeniable in the world around us that points to something greater.

Which is why the Bible was—and is—completely on point when Paul wrote the following in Romans 1:20, "For since the creation of the world God's invisible qualities—his eternal power and divine nature—have been clearly seen, being understood from what has been *made* [my emphasis], so that people are without excuse" (NIV). Because of this fact, that God's existence and invisible qualities can clearly be seen by what has been made, I believe everyone can come out of stage one on The Spiritual Taxonomy of Doubt. In fact, based on Romans 1:20, I believe everyone probably already has, they are just in denial. Eventually, though, this satanic doubt on whether or not God exists can evade us, and we can move up to stage two on the taxonomy: Which god to believe in?

For this stage, there is endless debate. With so many religions in the world, how can any one religion claim that they have the truth? People believe it's impossible for someone to have absolute truth. So, many will revert back to doubting God's existence altogether because there are too many similar options that all seem flawed. However, the lie that these people usually buy into is that all religions are relatively the same— which could not be farther from the truth.

The gospel of Jesus Christ flips all religions and

establishments on their heads; so much so that Jesus and His disciples were killed for what they were teaching. Jesus was essentially teaching that our salvation—and our relationship with God—is not a result of our own effort. We cannot earn our salvation based upon any number of works. The only way to God is through Jesus, God's Son. And through Jesus' intercession for us, we can have a real relationship with God— because He is the Door to God.

Another lie these people are buying into is that not a single religion *can* be true simply because there are so many "similar" options. Just because there are a lot of religions, this doesn't mean that none of them are true. Likewise, just because there are a lot of different hypotheses about how the universe came into existence, doesn't that none of them are correct. Through an honest and thorough investigation into each religion's philosophical, moral, historical, and scientific evidence we can come to a conclusion about which is objectively true or false, and to what degree.

It's amazing, though, returning to my previous point, that God *wants* to have a relationship with us, with our evil and sinful selves. This truth I will never fully understand, but I am incredibly grateful for it.

Nevertheless, some of us will come to know the Lord Jesus through His offer of grace upon grace. But when we do, we may find ourselves under the most intense, and unfortunately prolonged, spiritual attack that we will ever face. The Devil will try his absolute best to make us, especially when we are a new Christian, doubt our salvation. Because if the Devil can make you doubt your salvation, then he can keep you from spreading the gospel, and he can keep you from maturing spiritually. John Piper once said that if Satan can eat your faith and consume it and destroy it, then he doesn't care what else you do. Because if your faith is destroyed, then he can keep you from spreading the gospel, and he can keep other people stuck in stage one or two of The Spiritual Taxonomy of Doubt.

To doubt your salvation, though, is a more complicated issue than whether you said the "Salvation Prayer" or not. Jesus Christ Himself said in Mathew 7:21, "Not everyone who says to me, 'Lord, Lord,' will enter the kingdom of heaven, but only the one who does the will of my Father who is in heaven" (NIV). So, it's not simply that you said a prayer one time, but that God changed your heart, and that changed heart resulted in a changed life where you now desire to do the will of God.

People don't like to hear this verse, because they want to say a prayer and then go about living their life for themselves. But there's one problem with this attitude: A relationship with Christ is all about living your life for *Him*. This attitude is completely backwards to the gospel. We should desire to do the will of God—which is to give God glory by going to all the nations proclaiming the gospel. It's not that the good works save us, but it's that because we are truly saved that we want to do the good works.

Romans 10:9 says, "If you declare with your mouth, 'Jesus is Lord,' and believe in your heart that God raised him from the dead, you will be saved" (NIV). This is just as true as Mathew 7:21; however, if your life two years down the road from saying this prayer is exactly the same as it was before you "believed," then I would have serious doubts as to whether or not you really believed in your heart that God raised Jesus from the dead.

If God truly invaded your heart and he saved your soul, then the Holy Spirit is living inside of you, and your life will look different down the road. One way to tell if you have the Holy Spirit inside of yourself is to look back at your life since you allegedly gave it to Christ. Is there a difference? Do some heart searching to see if you have the fruit of the Spirit. Galatians 5:22-23 says, "But the fruit of the Spirit is love, joy, peace, patience, kindness, goodness, faithfulness, gentleness, self-control" (ESV).

To some degree, this fruit should be sprouting in your heart and life after you develop a relationship with God.[43] This isn't to say that you will have all of these overnight, but through years and years of getting to know God on a deeper and more intimate level, these will become more evident in your life over time.

Good trees bear good fruit. So the kind of fruit that you bear reveals the tree that you are connected to—and your tree limbs run straight through your heart. If you bear hate, anxiety, irritability, impatience, greed, murder, and adultery, then your fruit may be growing on a tree limb that is connected through a heart without Christ. If you bear love, joy, peace, patience, kindness, self-control, etc., then you probably are connected to the tree that is Christ. You see, Christ changes your heart first; then your heart sprouts fruit after. So the important thing to look at is the fruit.

It's sort of like looking for the evidence that an explosion occurred to start the universe into existence. If there is evidence to suggest the validity of the claim (such as the radiation afterglow and the expanding nature of the universe), then it is very likely that an explosion occurred. If there is evidence in your life that Christ invaded it (such as the way you live your life and the purpose behind it), then He probably did.

Nevertheless, many will stay in this level of the taxonomy for the rest of their lives. They will never see the work that the Holy Spirit has done in them. But I think it's time that we put this doubt behind us. That is, if we have seen the fruit of the Spirit manifested in our life; if we have put our faith in Jesus Christ; if we have repented of our sins, and if we have taken up our cross. Then, and only then, should we put this doubt behind us.

It's easier for me to put this doubt behind me now; mainly because I know Christ's blood has got my back, but it's something that I used to struggle with to an extreme degree. Even to the point where I would ask Christ into my heart multiple times in the same week. It's a horrible place to be, and the Devil knows that. He wants to keep you there for the rest of your life because he knows if he keeps you there you won't be serving God. Pray for God to get you out of this level of doubt so you can move forward.

One of the best ways to move forward is to get out of your comfort zone by doing something big for God. For instance, working at a summer Christian sports camp like Kanakuk. It is when you are way out of your comfort zone, and away from the regular routines of life, that you are truly challenged to rely on God. It is in these moments that you must depend on God the most. Additionally, it is also in these moments that you discover how much you appreciate your God-given purpose.

The next level of the taxonomy is the doubt over your purpose in life. Everyone is in such a rush to figure out their major for college and what they want to do for the rest of their lives. Then, when they actually get into their career position, they realize that their career doesn't satisfy them like they thought it would, and they go back to feeling depressed about their purpose.

It's really quite sad to me because finding your purpose is

very easy. According to the Bible, our purpose is simple: give God glory. The problem that arises later in life is a result of our believing in a misconception about life (that our careers are supposed to give us purpose and satisfy the deepest desires of our hearts). The truth is that your career isn't meant to give you purpose or satisfy the deepest desires of your heart. Only God can do either.

Isaiah 43:7 tells us that God made us for His glory; so let us use our life to do just that. To do this, we must understand that we do not own our lives; we are living on borrowed time bought with the blood of Jesus. It is time we use our lives to give Him glory by serving Him, spreading the Word, and living our lives in a way that shows the world we believe in Him.

It doesn't matter what career you pick, or what college you go to; what matters is *how* you go to college, and *how* you do your career. You should go to college with the purpose of serving God while you're there, an opportunity to witness to other people at your university. And with your career, the exact same thing. So don't get bogged down with the specific things of life; think more generally in terms of serving God, and you will be much more satisfied. You will climb out of the fourth stage of the taxonomy, and you will soon find yourself at the top level, experiencing peace. Philippians 4:6-7 says:

> Be anxious for nothing, but in everything by prayer and supplication with thanksgiving let your requests be made

known to God. And the peace of God, which surpasses all comprehension, will guard your hearts and your minds in Christ Jesus. (NASB)

Let God guard your heart and mind, and quit worrying so much. Instead of worrying, serve the Lord and let your worries be made known to Him. Then His peace *will* comfort you.

Sooner or later, through spiritual growth by the divine intervention of God, you will experience peace. This isn't to say that you won't fall back to any of the lower levels in this taxonomy, most people will fluctuate to some degree. But my hope is that we can stay in the peace stage for the majority of our lives. But it is important to remember that we experience this peace only through a relationship with Jesus Christ.

When all is said and done, this diagram is just a way to visualize the different levels of doubt that I believe the Devil uses to keep us in his grasp. He wants to keep you as low on this taxonomy as possible so he can keep you from doing that which will give you peace: serving your Creator.

There is so much noise in the world that the Devil uses to keep you down. Science just happens to be another area that he works through. My encouragement to you is to consider the things we have talked about in this section of the book. Look at the littlest things and the biggest things. Through them all you will see a common denominator of design, and you will climb out of the first level of the taxonomy. Hopefully, Christ will take you the rest of the way up.

Daniel Faucett

FLAMING ARROW #4

ANXIETY

Daniel Faucett

17

BE ANXIOUS FOR NOTHING

She woke up at the break of dawn, immediately to full awareness, and directly to a depressed mood. *What will my score on today's Biology test be?* She wondered as she got dressed and proceeded to the kitchen for breakfast. She began religiously re-reading her flashcards for the fifth time in eight hours. A late night beforehand had made her a little drowsy this morning. Steamy, her coffee was ready. *The perfect pick-me-up,* she thought as she poured a large mug.

She continued to review the terms. She was finally getting it. She could associate words with definitions; after all, that's all her teacher wanted, but she had no understanding of the material. She began to think about the test-review lecture in her mind. When the teacher drilled through the terms at 100 miles per hour. Examples for understanding were few and far between. The old professor forgot about the importance of understanding, or perhaps he no longer cared. Regardless, understanding of the material seemed absent on both ends.

She finished her pastry and drove to class. She drove quickly due to her testing anxiety. The entire way her palms became sweatier and sweatier. Upon arrival, her hands slipped off the steering wheel as she came to an abrupt stop. She wiped her hands off on her jeans before grabbing her book bag and heading to class. She paused outside the classroom door, took a deep breath, and walked inside with nothing but discomfort. It was time for her to be tested on her ability to remember 300 meaningless facts and word associations. It was Biology. The worst course for many students, and for her especially.

When she got home that afternoon, she walked right to her room and whipped out her laptop. She was dreading becoming aware of her score. She saw a notification on the online platform that an assignment had been graded. She paused, prayed to God, and finally clicked on the notification to see her score . . . 76%. She sunk into her seat in disappointment. A dark cloud rose over her as she felt the blood rush to her cheeks. Her eyes began to water, her vision blurred. She was afraid to show her score to her parents, or to her friends and classmates. She had already forgotten the word associations that she had memorized, and now it was time for her to begin reading the online presentations and meaningless terms that would be associated with the next test. *Will I be able to do better on the next exam?* She thought as she began to cry. It was not that she didn't care; it was not that she didn't prepare; it was simply that she was not good at memorizing loads of extraneous information.

Unfortunately, this is the testing experience for many people in today's world. Rather in high school or college. We are given study guides and lectures, but many instructors do not teach for understanding. They teach for memorization, and many students are not good at memorizing extraneous cognitive loads of information.

Benjamin Franklin once said, "Tell me and I forget, teach me and I may remember, involve me and I learn."[1] Sadly, many teachers do not involve students; they just try to blurt through hundreds of terms and expect students to bottle them up and throw them out on a test. The woman in our example was never given a chance to be involved; if she was, then she probably would have understood the material enough to remember it for her exam. I'm not saying all of this to bash teachers and the way they do their jobs, I'm just trying to show you the experience that most students have.

Be Anxious For Nothing

My point in saying all of this is to give you an illustration of how the Devil works. He uses testing anxiety to weigh down the hearts of students. Many of my campers at Kanakuk felt overwhelmed by the pressure to do well in the classroom, on standardized assessments, and in sports. But why does the Devil want these kids to feel anxious? Simple, because God does *not* want them to feel anxious. Satan always is the opposite of God in his spiritual intentions and goals—because he is in opposition *to* God.

In fact, God commands us not to be anxious at all. According to Philippians 4:6-7:

> Be anxious for nothing, but in everything by prayer and supplication, with thanksgiving, let your requests be made known to God; and the peace of God, which surpasses all understanding, will guard your hearts and minds through Christ Jesus. (NKJV)

We often try to solve our anxiety problems on our own with various escapes. Some people workout, play basketball, read books, or listen to music to cope. Others get so overwhelmed by the pressures of life that they will resort to drinking alcohol, dipping tobacco, smoking weed, or smoking cigarettes to relieve the anxiety. Everyone is different, and some peoples' escapes are far less damaging to their lives than others. Nevertheless, they are all avenues by which to cope with anxiety. For me, it's playing basketball.

But here in Philippians, God is telling us something very different than taking our anxiety into our own hands by playing basketball or smoking weed. It's telling us to put our anxiety in God's hands. The first thing we should do to relieve anxiety is talk to God, not participate in a desired activity. As soon as we feel stress about anything that is going on in our lives, we should make those needs known to Him. Scripture tells us that the peace of God will guard our hearts and our minds in Christ Jesus if we do this.

I have felt God's presence overwhelmingly when it comes to this area. Whether I have been anxious about school, or struggling with a particular sin, God has given me peace when I have asked Him for it. Make your requests known to God, and you too can feel the peace come over you.

There's a huge difference here in what we naturally try to do to cope with anxiety, and what God is commanding us to do. God is telling us to completely let go, while the Devil plays on our natural desires to dance with our thoughts. Satan wants us to go play basketball, drink or smoke so that we can marinate in our anxieties. He has no intention of leading us away from them; he just wants us to ignore them until they can resurface later and cause immense pain. In this sense, he is the king of ignorance. However, God is the king of peace, and He will give you peace in exchange for your anxieties. (Sound like a fair trade?)

This verse also tells us the peace of God surpasses all understanding. I have found this to be very true. Whenever I actually give my anxieties to Him, I experience peace, but I can't explain how it works. I guess it's hard to understand because it seems to go against logic. Usually when we have a problem, we just think about it long and hard until we find an answer. This is a fine process for some things; however, if you struggle with anxiety you know this doesn't work at all. God knows that if you struggle with anxiety, then you do not need to overthink your problems. You need to give them to Him, and He can give you a peace where you then can approach your problems in an anxiety-free manner.

Give Your Problems to God

But how do we give our problems to God? This passage in Philippians tells us that we should make our requests known to Him by prayer, supplication, and thanksgiving. We cannot give our problems to God if we do not pray to Him. If we just keep them bottled up we will never let them go. But, first and foremost, we must acknowledge the God of the universe in humble prayer.

Once we are in prayer, we should make our supplications (or requests) known to Him. Of course, God already knows what we need before we ever ask. However, God still commands us to make our requests known to Him for a reason. Perhaps He wants us to make our requests known to Him in prayer because it is a relationship-building experience. It's sort of like the relationship between a son and his earthly father. When a son asks his father for something, it can be a humbling and relationship-building experience. If a son never needed to ask his father for anything, then he probably wouldn't be a very humble person (since he would have pride that he was able to accomplish everything on his own). Additionally, they wouldn't speak very much because there wouldn't be as many reasons to do so. Of course, there are a million other reasons for discourse, but it seems like this one aspect has a large impact on the long-term nature of the father-son relationship.

Therefore, my conclusion is that God wants us to make our requests known to Him in prayer for three reasons: (1) He wants to keep us humble, (2) He wants to build up our relationship with Him, and (3) He wants to *perpetuate* our relationship with Him.

The third aspect to this passage is thanksgiving. But what should we thank Him for? Perhaps we should give Him thanks for the things He has already given us; such as salvation and friendship from the Son, wisdom from the Father, and peace from the Holy Spirit. Or, we should thank Him in advance for

His infinite sovereignty. That He has a divine plan and that everything happens for a reason.

With everything considered, I believe this passage in Philippians to be one of the most applicable and powerful passages in all of scripture. It flips our method of dealing with our anxiety on its head. We no longer should overthink our problems and stress. We should no longer seek escapes. We should make our requests concerning our problems known to God through prayer, supplication, and thanksgiving. When we do this, the peace of God *will* guard our hearts in Christ Jesus our Lord.

18

WORRY

Jesus once stood atop a mountain and delivered powerful words. These words have now become some of the most cherished statements in all of human history. Thankfully, we can find a record of these words in Mathew chapter six, in what is commonly referred to as "The Sermon on the Mount." Jesus, in verse twenty-five, tells us:

> For this reason I say to you, do not be worried about your life, as to what you will eat or what you will drink; nor for your body, as to what you will put on. Is not life more than food, and the body more than clothing? (NASB)

The most obvious conclusion we can draw from this verse is

that we should not be worried about our most basic needs. Rather, we should live a lifestyle where we don't worry about them at all. But what about things besides our most basic needs—our wants—are we permitted to worry with regard to them? Well, wants can be very different for people in different financial situations, and our different perspectives may cause us to justify worry in our own ways.

Imagine three different people: President Donald Trump, a middleclass teacher, and a homeless man. All three of these individuals have very different wants. But, their basic needs are exactly the same. All of these men need food and water, and depending on the temperatures from which they reside, shelter and clothing. However, when it comes to wants, we probably can see a lot of differences. The wants of Donald Trump are probably mostly political: regulation reduction, tax reform, and free market healthcare reform. The wants of a middle-class teacher are more small scale: a good retirement plan, savings for his daughter's college tuition, and a membership to a nice golf course. The wants of a homeless man are even more humble: a warm meal, a soda, and perhaps even a minimum wage job. Unfortunately, it's not just the case that these people want these things; in addition, they *worry* about these things. Each of their wants, however different they may be, causes each person to justify worry in their own way. A homeless man worries about getting a job, a middleclass man worries about retirement, and the president worries about passing legislation. And that's precisely the problem for all of us: we don't just want, we worry. Everyone does it, but the question remains, is worry permitted in scripture?

I believe when Jesus is commanding us not to worry about what we will eat, drink, or wear, He is talking about more than our basic needs. Think about it, if we're not supposed to worry about the most vital things pertaining to our survival (food, water, and clothes), why should we be allowed to worry about less-important things like retirement, tax plans, and potential jobs? For this reason, I believe we are also commanded not to worry about our wants because they are less important in many ways to our needs. So it is neither wants nor needs that can justify worry. Whether your wants are small or large is irrelevant to this command.

Of course, there is a difference in worry and preparation. Just because we are commanded not to worry, doesn't mean we are commanded not to plan wisely. Saving for your daughter's college tuition, applying for a good job, and trying to reduce government waste are all noble endeavors. Careful, meticulous planning should be ensued to ensure these matters are taken care of appropriately. The only difference is that worry should never cross your mind when doing so because God wants you to live a worry-free lifestyle.

Furthermore, I believe it to be a great misconception that

you must worry in order to plan. In truth, worry and preparation are two completely separate things that should not be amalgamated. Naturally, worry can motivate good planning, but it is sort of like motivating someone to do work by threatening them with a whip. It's just not a healthy way to do things. It may produce results, but it costs a great deal of pain.

Concerning the major theme of this verse, Jesus is telling us that life is more than just fulfilling our basic needs. But if life is more than survival, what is it all about? What is the higher calling of the human race? Some people may think that our higher calling is to simply pursue our wants at all costs.

When I was in high school, the popular term to motivate a want-driven lifestyle was *YOLO*—which was an acronym for *you only live once*. Unfortunately for the masses who paraded this term as they performed all kinds of debauchery, it is just not true. You may only live once on Earth, but you will live forever in one of two places for eternity—this truth, in contrast, is quite *un*popular. There is much more to life than following our sinful desires.

Now, as selfish as this may sound, it is true to some degree that we should spend our lives pursuing our wants. Psalm 37:4 tells us, "Delight yourself in the Lord, and he will give you the desires of your heart" (ESV). People often have a misunderstanding of this verse because it seems like the Bible is telling us that God is going to give us everything we want.

I've heard people say things (facetiously) such as, "According to this verse, God should give me a brand-new car!" The Bible is telling us that God is going to give us the desires of our hearts; but if one genuinely wants a full understanding of what the Bible is actually saying, you must look at the entire verse. What comes before the part about "getting" your desires are the words "Delight yourself in the Lord." If we first delight ourselves in the Lord, then yes, God will give us the desires of our hearts. But in order to receive the desires of our hearts, we must do this very important thing first.

But what does it mean to delight ourselves in the Lord?

To delight in something would be to find great pleasure in it. You could delight yourself in cookies by eating a lot of them—which would provide great pleasure. Or, more importantly, you could delight yourself in your family by spending quality time with them—which would also provide pleasure. So when we delight ourselves in the Lord, we are finding pleasure in Him. We are setting aside quality time to pursue intimacy with our Creator. And to truly delight ourselves in the God of the universe, I believe we must place Him above everything *in* the universe. We must let Jesus Christ rule the throne of our heart. Above all books, movies, technologies, friends, religious routines, and even family. Once we have truly placed God above all other things in our lives, we can experience great intimacy with Him, and then God can fill our hearts with certain desires. It is these desires, that come as a result of delighting ourselves in Jesus Christ, that God fulfills. (I think you can easily imagine how God-given desires would be much different than receiving a brand-new car.) Therefore, the desires that God wants to fulfill in our lives are the desires that He places in our hearts when we delight ourselves in Him. Our desires simply become His desires.

A few months ago I was at McDonald's having some coffee with my pastor, Todd Borders, and we were discussing this very topic with regards to career decisions. He told me bluntly, "If you have delighted yourself in the Lord, then go to the college you *want* to go to." It sounds like a liberal mindset, but it's very biblical. If your desire to go to a specific college is reinforced because of you having delighted yourself in the Lord, then you can be fully confident that that particular school is the place where God wants you to go. When you're wondering who you should marry, the scenario is exactly the same—who do you *want* to marry? Delight yourself in the Lord, by placing Him above all else, and then let Him lead you to marry the person He wants you to marry—simply by following your new desires.

This passage reveals to us that even the biggest decisions, such as who we will marry and what we will major in, still do not justify worry. No matter how big the decision may be, or how important the want may seem, they do not justify worry.

After all, the Word tells us that we cannot add one hour of time to our lives by being worried (Matthew 6:27). Think about it, worrying is just time wasted. For example, if you're worried about dying, worrying will not only shorten your life due to increased stress, but it will also make the time you have left more miserable and unsatisfying.

In addition, worrying doesn't actually cause anything to get accomplished, it just makes the accomplishment process less enjoyable. And not only is worrying time wasted and unproductive, but it is also completely unnecessary. If worrying was necessary, then God would command us to worry! He would also give us guidelines in the Bible on how to worry. However, God knows that we can enjoy our lives more, become healthier, give Him more glory, and even become more successful in life when we get rid of worry.

But now that we have clarified needs and wants—and that we shouldn't worry about either—we can see clearly the higher calling that Jesus is referring to in the Sermon on the Mount. Our higher calling is to go out and make disciples, baptizing them in the name of the Father, the Son, and the Holy Spirit (Mathew 28:19); which consequently gives God immense glory (Isaiah 43:7). They're the two big missions that are really one in the same: give God glory, and do that by making disciples. And the motivation to pursue these missions comes from the desires that God places in our hearts.

Now, it is not a basic biological need to witness to other people. Of course, you can survive a lifetime without ever doing it. Hence, it must be a want (or a desire) to witness to other people. And this desire should come as a result of having delighted ourselves in the Lord. That's how we know if we are truly delighting ourselves in the Lord: if the desires of our heart point back to scripture. Do we desire to share the gospel with the masses? Do we desire to marry a woman who wants to live a Christ-centered life? Do we desire to become a part of a body of believers? Do we desire to go out and help the needy and the poor? When we analyze our new desires, we can often times quite easily gauge whether they have been placed there by our Lord Jesus Christ. So in a sense, we do live a want-driven lifestyle. We follow the wants and desires and pure satisfaction that God places in our hearts, and doing so gives us great joy and God great glory.[2]

In verse thirty-four Jesus ends this passage with the following words, "So do not worry about tomorrow; for tomorrow will care for itself. Each day has enough trouble of its own" (NASB). Have you ever started thinking about all the things in your future that you should be worried about? Like getting into college; getting scholarships; making good grades; graduating with a good resume so you can get a good job; marrying a good Christian woman; raising your kids. Oh, wait, now you gotta think about how you're going to pay for your kids' college expenses. Before you know it, you will be worrying about things that have very little relevance to your life at this very moment. You will be overwhelmed with worry and anxiety. Each day has enough trouble of its own. While it's ok to pray and plan for our future, and our kids' futures, we shouldn't worry about our future needs and wants.

The takeaway for this chapter: don't worry about anything. Don't worry about wants, needs, or anything that may come up in the future. We are commanded not to worry about these things, so it's time to live a worry-free lifestyle. It will be more enjoyable, and most importantly it will give God more glory.

Daniel Faucett

19

WEIGHT ROOM

Perhaps you don't have a worrying problem, except when life gets hard. When life throws you a curveball of persecution, illness, or financial instability. It is in these times that you become anxious and worry. When you realize you are sixty thousand dollars in debt after graduation. Or when you realize that you are going to have chemotherapy, or perhaps even double-bypass heart surgery. It is very easy to sink into anxiety in these situations—it is even easier to justify it. However, even in the darkest of times, we should not be anxious because there are no exceptions to the biblical guidelines concerning anxiety and worry.

Psalm 34:19 says, "Many are the afflictions of the righteous, But the LORD delivers him out of them all" (NASB). I believe you will come out of your afflictions because of this very promise. Our God is the *Deliverer*, and He clearly promises to deliver us. It may not be until death, but eventually we will be brought out of our earthly afflictions. Unfortunately, this verse doesn't say when or how we will come out of our afflictions, so we are left with a lot of uncertainty. But this uncertainty is no reason to be anxious.

When we are in a season of tribulation in our life, how are we to act if we are not permitted to be anxious? According to Romans 5:3-5:

> And not only this, but we also *exult* [my emphasis] in our tribulations, knowing that tribulation brings about perseverance; and perseverance, proven character; and proven character, hope; and hope does not disappoint, because the love of God has been poured out within our hearts through the Holy Spirit who was given to us. (NASB)

We are to *exult* in our tribulations. (Exult most nearly means rejoice!) So we are truly to rejoice in our trials and tribulations. We should be happy that we are going through them because we know we will be stronger on the other side.

John Piper once gave a sermon on this very topic, and he made an analogy between the theme of this verse and the use of a bicep. When you lift a weight with your bicep it hurts. It is hard to lift that weight and curl it up from your waist to your chest. However, repetition after repetition, day after day, your muscle grows stronger. Through the trial of working out—something that is undesirable to do for most people—we see results on the other side. This is synonymous with our faith and our character. When we go through trials, tribulations, and persecutions; we develop character. Just like when we work out, we develop stronger muscles.

Many times in my life I have been denied things that I wanted. When I was a junior in high school, I was not chosen to be a part of the starting five line-up in basketball. I worked hard the entire off season. Blood, sweat, and tears. I was naturally frustrated when I didn't get rewarded the way I thought I deserved. However, God did not want me to have a negative attitude. God worked through me in those times to develop character in me. He taught me that you do not always get what you want. Sometimes, you must take a backseat behind others. Even when you think you're better, it doesn't matter because you are not in control. God was in control of whether or not I started that year, not my coach. God had bigger character-development plans for me my junior year than simply scoring a lot of points, or having a good assist-to-turnover ratio. Through my trials, and through my disappointments, God developed in me character; and that character is far more valuable to me now than better basketball stats.

First Corinthians 10:13 tells us:

No temptation has overtaken you that is not common to man. God is faithful, and he will not let you be tempted beyond your ability, but with the temptation he will also provide the way of escape, that you may be able to endure it. (ESV)

God will allow us to be tempted, sometimes to an extreme degree, but never beyond what we are able to endure. God may allow Satan to drag us down into the dirt, but never too far. God knows when to stop Satan, and He allows this to happen to develop character, perseverance, and hope in our hearts.

Satan is sort of like our weight room. We all work out in this room while we are on Earth. And through working out in this room (through experiencing trials, temptations, and tribulations), God is able to strengthen us beyond what we would be able to be strengthened without this intense resistance. Likewise, when we work out without weights, we only get so strong; it is when we pile on *extra* resistance that we start to become *extra* strong. Satan's influence in our world is that extra resistance, and through the power of Christ we are able to endure and achieve great perseverance, strength, character, and hope.

We walk a fine line, though, between this resistance, and

what we are able to endure. As we grow stronger, I think God often allows Satan to add more resistance to our lives (but God never allows him to add too much). However, if more weights were never added, then we would never get stronger. It's not fun at first when you add more resistance to your workout routine, but in the end, you are a stronger person and you are glad that you did. I believe it is the same way with the struggles God allows to happen in our lives.

As John Piper says, God wants that bicep to be strong for the future hard situations we will encounter in our lives. There are things that I learned from my junior year of basketball that will give me an incredible opportunity to reach out to future players who are frustrated with their positions on their teams. I will understand their situations better and on a deeper level because I've been there before. My spiritual bicep will be strong enough to help lift others up out of their situations. I will also be prepared if I get in that type of situation again.

This is another reason why God allows us to go through these tough circumstances. Sometimes He wants to walk us through a tough situation so that we can then witness to others who go through similar struggles. We can share with them how God was the reason we made it through our tough times. Second Corinthians 1:4 says that God comforts us in all our afflictions so that we can comfort others who are in any affliction. This shows that the comfort God gives us in our afflictions is the same comfort with which we should give others in their afflictions.

This is a clear picture of how God works through us. He allows us to be persecuted and to go through trials; he allows us to have afflictions. But these develop in us a sense of God's comfort, with which we can then transfer to others.

So are we to be anxious under certain circumstances? May it never be! Let us rejoice in God's comfort, discipline, and allowed tribulations, just as body builders rejoice in the resistance of lifting weights. I believe that over time, we too can fall in love with the process of spiritual strength-building.

Five Flaming Arrows

Daniel Faucett

FLAMING ARROW #5

DEPRESSION

Daniel Faucett

20

DEPRESSION

Suicide is the tenth leading cause of death in the United States.[4] Each year 44,965 Americans die by suicide, and for every suicide there are twenty-five attempts.[4] Up to 15% of those who are clinically depressed die by suicide[1] (compare that to the national suicide rate of less than a fraction of one percent). So in other words, from the data we find a correlation between depression and suicide. And this doesn't come as a surprise, when someone is depressed they have no sense of purpose; they are emotionally destroyed, and they feel that they would be better off if they were not living anymore. But what is it that causes depression?

I believe it is the spiritual forces of darkness that causes people to go into depression. Satan is out to kill, steal, and destroy; so depression is just another avenue by which he can accomplish that goal. In a sense, the Devil is quite clever in that he works through feelings of depression and suicide in order to achieve this destruction. If the Devil can get you to kill yourself as a result of depression; then he has likely sealed you for eternity in Hell—or if you were saved by the blood of Christ, then he has taken you out of the spiritual battle on Earth. That is why I think it's the Devil who tries to produce depression and suicidal thoughts in the hearts of men. He knows they are the best mechanisms by which to keep people from winning souls to Christ.

I have dealt with depression personally. You see, I was a very bipolar kid. One minute I would be having a grand ole time, and then the next minute I would be threatening to kill myself. At my lowest point, I was standing on the top of our garage, which had a near twenty-foot-high gable roof, and I was threatening to jump off in a fit of tears. When we were younger it was just seen as a kid over reacting—and that was probably more or less true—but the emotions were dark and spiritual. As I grew older, however, I drifted into a more emotionally stable and stagnant position.

By the time I got to high school, I had a very consistent mood. Unfortunately, it just wasn't a very good one. I struggled with feelings of depression that were so consistent they scared me.

I knew these feelings were different than when I was younger because they never left me. Even when I would have joyful moments, these feelings would still creep up at the bottom of my heart. I believe it was partly because I was dealing with the conviction of my sin on a scale I had never felt before in my life. I don't know if it was the Devil telling me I wasn't good enough, or the Holy Spirit opening my eyes to my own sin, but either way I was depressed because of how evil of a person I had let myself become. It really is a depressing realization: to discover that your whole life you've been living a lie.

My whole life I had thought that I was a Christian, but I was really just putting on a facade of Christianity. I wanted to look like a Christian. I wanted to go to church. I wanted to have all the right answers. I wanted to go to Heaven. But I didn't want to surrender my life to Christ. There was a big difference in what Christianity actually is all about, and what my life looked like on the inside, and I think that is what truly caused me to become depressed.

One night when I was fifteen, my convictions became overwhelming. I was disgusted with myself and the sin that consumed me. I talked to Jesus. I surrendered my life to Him. I was done living a double life where I pretended to be a

Christian in public, yet behind closed doors (and in my heart) I was no different than someone without the Spirit. I asked Jesus Christ to take the burden of my sin away from me.

Before that night, I had asked Jesus into my heart probably a hundred times. However, the other times I never felt the burden of my sin lifted. I never felt any surer of my salvation, and I never desired to follow in Jesus' footsteps. This time, though, it was very different. I immediately felt a heart change. I wasn't on an emotional high. I wasn't trying to walk up to the alter to get recognition. It was just me and God and an intensely spiritual encounter.

Before when I asked Jesus into my heart, I never knew why I did it other than that I didn't want to go to Hell. Which is something that I think draws a lot of people to Christ. It's not such a bad thing because Hell is a real place, and it should cause you to consider Jesus. However, my problem was that I didn't want to change my life, follow Jesus, or surrender my idols. Up until this point I had not yet truly been convicted of these things. I wanted to stay indulgent in my personal sin for the rest of my life, and then at the end I wanted to go to Heaven. I just wanted to use Jesus as a means to an end.

But this time, I finally recognized that I was in the wrong for the way I had treated Jesus. I needed Him to change things for me, and that is what Christ did that very day. I needed Him to not only clean me up, but to take me as I was. I needed Him to clean my dark heart that no one else knew about.

He changed my heart from the inside out. My desires began to change, and my actions slowly but surely followed. God may change you immediately, bit it takes a lot of time to grow you. So I am still growing to this day. While I do have setbacks all the time, I hope I can steadily and genuinely pursue Jesus for the rest of my life through the strength that only He can provide.

After my spiritual transformation, my depression left me for a while. I felt the assurance of my salvation. I knew God had genuinely invaded my heart. I felt the peace that comes from a daily relationship with the Creator of the universe. However, after two years I had begun to doubt my salvation again. The spiritual fire I had once experienced became a dim light. The Devil began to whisper to me that I was kidding myself if I thought God had *really* saved me. He began to point to my shortcomings—in the manner he always does—by drawing my attention to every act of disobedience.

If you haven't noticed this in your own life yet, you will. The Devil always tries to make you doubt your salvation—as I discussed in the Spiritual Taxonomy of Doubt. Because if he can make you doubt your salvation, then he will keep you from serving God. And if Satan can keep you from serving God, he can by default keep you serving himself. I don't believe there is a middle ground. You are either with Christ or against Him.

Nevertheless, my depression returned as a result of this doubt. I felt like I was without a purpose. It was like nothing I did ultimately mattered, and this made me very unsatisfied. I was very good about putting on a face in front of my friends and family; however, deep down inside of my heart were groanings too solemn for me to reveal. There were only two people who knew how I really felt: Bailey, and God.

When I told Bailey about my feelings of depression, she soon brought me two notecards with a long list of Bible verses on them. These verses were meant to provide me with spiritual encouragement. It was just what the doctor ordered. This was probably the most comforting and encouraging gift from another person on this earth I have ever received. It hit the deepest recesses of my soul. (After all, the Bible doe say that the Word never returns void.)

It was like God reached down from Heaven into the bottom of my heart with a shovel, and began to scoop up a pile of gravel that was weighing down my heart. With every verse that I meditated on, it was like God was throwing out the doubts about my salvation scoop by scoop. And not only was He throwing out the doubts, but He was filling in the space with His purpose for my life, and His incomparable love for my soul. It was at that point that I realized that God can truly work through others to minister to you.

This gift represented that someone on this earth had

sympathy for my feelings, for my hurts. It pointed me right back to the scriptures, and the verses were directly applicable to my situation. In the next few pages I will discuss these verses that Bailey shared with me my senior year of high school. I hope they give you the same peace they gave me.

Philippians 4:8 was the first on the list. It told me to dwell on what is true, honorable, right, pure, lovely, of good repute, excellent, and worthy of praise. I realized our mindsets should not be consumed with negativity, like my mind had been for so long.

Here in Philippians, the Bible is telling us to meditate on what is good. While we should workout our salvation with fear and trembling, and we should examine our own heart, we also should look to the Bible verses that give us the assurance of our salvation. We should dwell on the promises of God, because the promises are meant for His children. The warnings of God's wrath are meant for the sons of disobedience, not the followers of Jesus Christ. For example, 1st Thessalonians 5:9-10 says, "For God has not destined us for wrath, but for obtaining salvation through our Lord Jesus Christ, who died for us, so that whether we are awake or asleep, we will live together with Him" (NASB).

The second verses given to me were Psalm 40:1-2, which accurately depict our relationship with God through Christ. David wrote these beautiful verses thousands of years ago, yet what he had to say could not be more applicable to our lives in the twenty-first century:

> I waited patiently for the Lord; And He inclined to me and heard my cry. He brought me up out of the pit of destruction, out of the miry clay, And He set my feet upon a rock making my footsteps firm. (NASB)

I no longer had to worry about my salvation because God had already picked me up from the pit of destruction. He had saved me according to Romans 10:9, and He had brought me up into newness of life. Not only had He saved my soul, but now he had placed me upon the Rock that is Jesus Christ. This Rock from which I would stand for the rest of my life. The Rock of Salvation, Peace, and absolute Truth.

First Peter 5:7 says that we should cast all our anxiety on God, because He cares for us. Such a simple verse, but so powerful and applicable to where I was in my life. Here God is simply telling us that He cares for us and wants to take our burdens on Himself—which is exactly what He did on the Cross. He wants what's best for us; just like any good father should. Whether you're dealing with depression, or anxiety, He wants to take those struggles upon Himself.

John 16:33 says, "These things I have spoken to you, so that in Me you may have peace. In the world you have tribulation, but take courage; I have overcome the world" (NASB). I had thought that my life was hard, but God pointed me back to His Son's life. *He* lived the ultimate life of persecution, even up until the moments of His crucifixion and death. There was no emotional distress that *I* could go through that would compare to Christ's suffering; I was acting like a child spiritually by being depressed and anxious all the time. Therefore, I had no room to complain about anything that I went through in my life. I had no room to dwell on negativity. God wanted me to dwell on His Son's words so that in Him I would have peace. After meditating on these verses, I began to do that more often, and my depression left me.

There was always the thought in the back of my head, however, that perhaps God wouldn't always protect me. I thought that the Devil could ruin me if he really wanted to, spiritually and physically by attacking me. But then, I came to a verse Bailey had put on the notecards she gave me. It was Romans 8:38-39:

> For I am convinced that neither death, nor life, nor angels, nor principalities, nor things present, nor things to come, nor powers, nor height, nor depth, nor any other created thing, will be able to separate us from the love of God, which is in Christ Jesus our Lord. (NASB)

This provided me immense comfort: to really know how much God has my back in the spiritual realm and in the physical world.

I believe that the spiritual realm was having a battle over my soul, and God completely and utterly won. He showed me that I no longer needed to be depressed because He had saved me, and His love cannot be separated from me. Not even Satan himself, or demons, can separate me from this love He has for me.

God was speaking to me through these verses, and my life has not been the same since I meditated on them. Before, I wasn't focusing in on God's promises; like His promise of salvation or His promise to be my source of strength. I was focused in on an emotional feeling. And we all know there's a huge difference between our *feelings* about God's promises, and God's actual *promises*. (Thankfully, our ephemeral thoughts and feelings do not void God's promises!) I thought that I had to have an emotional feeling to be truly saved. Since I was having depressed feelings very often, I thought I had never been saved. This mindset could not have been farther from the truth. God started a relationship with me on that day when I was fifteen and I asked Him to be the Lord of my life. From that point on, it was a steady growth into intimacy with God. This intimacy with God doesn't happen overnight; it happens through time spent together—just like any relationship. Sadly, when I was seventeen and eighteen, I had not spent time with God like I should have; thus, I felt disconnected from Him. I had not meditated on His Word; thus, I felt like I didn't know who He was or what He valued. However, regardless of how I felt, His promises were still true, and His salvation never left me; I had simply run from Him and forgotten about our relationship. Through reading these verses, though, I got back on track, my depression left me, and I began to foster my relationship with God once again through Jesus Christ.

For me, the spiritual victory in the end was God's. Unfortunately, sometimes Satan wins in this area of people's lives. Satan makes people feel so negative about themselves that they do drastic things to cope—some even go through with killing themselves, or they stay under chronic depression for the rest of their lives. I'm here to tell you that God doesn't want you to live like that. He doesn't want you to be a slave to depression. He wants you to have an intimate relationship with Him that results in peace and satisfaction.

Second Peter 3:9 tells us that God wishes for none to perish, but for all to come to repentance. When God says *all*, He means it. The only question is how long will you ignore His promises and His grace? How long will you focus on what the Devil is whispering into your ears? Of course, you should honestly examine your own heart; however, when the examination clearly points to Christ's presence in your life, why are you still waiting to be confident in your salvation? It's time to rise out of the "miry clay" in your own heart and mind, because, in reality, you already have!

Here is a comprehensive list of the verses that were given

to me to help me with depression; I'm sure that they will be able to help you as well:

Philippians 4:8
Deuteronomy 31:8
Psalm 27:14, 34:17, 40:1-3, 42:11, 43:5
John 16:33
Jeremiah 17:7
Proverbs 16:3, 12-5
Romans 8:38-39
Isaiah 41:10
1st Peter 4:12-13
2nd Peter 2:9
2nd Corinthians 1:3-4

21

THE WORLD DOESN'T SATISFY

My day always starts out with a hot cup of black coffee. Then, I read a little bit in the Bible and say my morning prayers. From there I usually get dressed, eat breakfast, and set out to start my day. Usually, the day is full of doing things to satisfy my own needs and wants. Of course, I need to work to make money to pay for my family's wellbeing, but I don't need to spend thirty minutes of my day cruising through online technology deals. I need to eat to stay alive, but I don't need to eat two helpings or dessert. What I'm getting at is that the majority of my day is filled with time I spend trying to satisfy my own needs and wants.

I'd like to say that I'm a super Christian. That I only do things for God, but that would be a bad lie. If you know me, then you know I'm not perfect, and you also know I do most things for myself. We all do, Christians are not above anyone else. The only difference is that the Christian should be convicted by the Holy Spirit and should at least feel bad about it. What we do with that conviction, though, is largely up to the individual. And I wish that I spent more time listening to that conviction and then doing things for God when He calls me to do them. Nevertheless, the problem I want to address in this chapter is the problem of satisfaction. We should all ask ourselves, "What are the things we do to seek satisfaction, and how do those things measure up?"

For instance, as I'm writing this chapter I'm still a little wet from the shower I took after my intramural basketball game. A game that I felt excited about all day, and one that I even practiced for. However, at the end of a full night of basketball, teamwork, and even a win, all I can feel is an emptiness inside of myself. I don't know what it is, but it's definitely there. For some reason, it's always been there after I play basketball. My wife will tell you that I often come home from the gym depressed, even if I won all the games that I played in, and even if I played great myself. For some odd reason, I often feel an emptiness when I play the sport. And it's peculiar because basketball is the most fun, exciting, and competitive sport I've ever taken part in. (Heck, I've playing it since I was six years old for a reason.) But even still, I can't escape this emptiness I feel after I've played basketball for a day.

I think I keep playing because I always have had this desire to put my competitiveness out there, and to be noticed by people. We all want to be noticed, and it feels really nice when we can go do something and be congratulated for it. I like basketball because I'm good enough at it to be noticed by others when I play. And to be honest, it feels good to be the first pick when I play pick-up basketball at the gym. But at the end of the day, I'm empty.

I guess basketball makes me feel empty because I use it in a secular manner. It has the same effect as the coffee, it gives me something in return. Coffee gives me a caffeine rush, basketball gives me an ego rush, work gives me money, and everything else I do during the day gives me something different. At my most basic level, almost everything I do is directly or indirectly done for myself.

Even when I do good things for other people, I am really doing them for myself. I may say that what I am doing for someone else is out of the goodness of my own heart, but often times, I do it just because I want a "thank you." Or, rather than a "thank you," I may want others to simply see me as a good person. A really nice, humble, virtuous, or generous person. I can honestly say that I've done very few "good deeds" outside of these reasons. I also often do good things because I want to give Christians a good name. I want to sit down at the end of the day and say, "See, Christians are better than ... fill in the blank!" So it seems like most of my good deeds can really be broken down into sinful motivating factors such as pride, over competitiveness, or a desire to be admired.

The times that you haven't thought about the good deeds you took part in are probably the times that you actually have done something for the Lord. In other words, if you don't think about how good of a person you are after you do something, then you may have just done something for God. When we are truly doing something for the sole purpose of giving God glory, then He should be the only thing that is on our minds. We shouldn't be dwelling on our own humbleness, kindness, or generosity. We shouldn't be dwelling on what we look like. We should only be focused on how we can follow God's calling and how we can give Him glory in doing so. The issue with living in the world is that it offers us so many things that attempt to satisfy the desires of our hearts. The world even offers us a secular humility! But it's a false humility. It offers us the ability to be generous, but it's a false generosity. They are false character qualities because they are based on getting something in return.

True, God-given generosity expects nothing in return. True humility neither expects nor demands attention from others.

You see, if we think ourselves humble or generous, we are probably neither. Your awareness of those characteristics can become so great that they drown out the actual characteristics themselves. When your awareness grows bigger, then what has actually grown bigger is your pride, not your genuine humility or generosity.

Some people think that having these qualities will satisfy the desire of their heart to be a good person. But what you will soon realize is that what you actually have received from the world is pride masked in a false humility and a false generosity.

Now, I say all this because in this world we can develop many riches, and not just material ones. We gain the riches of money, but also humility, generosity, interpersonal skills, family, and even friends. All of these can be developed in the world without having God at the center of our lives. The only problem is that all of these things will develop in a twisted fashion. And, at the end of the day, all we have is an empty feeling. Or at least, that's all I have when I put myself at the foundation of these riches. No level of generosity or humility has ever satisfied me on the inside. No amount of hanging with friends, playing basketball, or the earning of money has ever made me feel a smidge better on the inside. The satisfaction of my soul, in the deepest recesses of my very being, is lacking on days when I have all these things. Yes, these things mentioned above make me excited and motivated at times, but there is still an overwhelming emptiness that I can't escape at the end of a day filled with their presence.

Tom Brady once said in an interview following his third Super Bowl victory, "Why do I have three Super Bowl rings and ... and still think there's something greater out there for me? I mean, maybe a lot of people would say 'hey man this is what it is,' I've reached my goal, my dream, my life is ... me, I think 'God, it's gotta be more than this.'" The interviewer then asked, "What's the answer?" Brady replied with, "I wish I knew. I wish I knew."[7]

The empty feeling I come home with after a day of basketball is the same feeling that Tom Brady seems to have after winning something much bigger than my backyard pick-up games. Tom Brady is in the big leagues, so if you think my experience is only unsatisfying because of the level at which I play then I would argue otherwise based on Tom Brady and countless other stars who have been at the top. It doesn't matter what level you play at, or even what you are doing every day, all that matters is why you do the things you do. Both myself and Tom Brady have tried to fill a hole in our hearts with something other than Jesus Christ. Even though I am a born-again believer, I still try to satisfy my desire for God with so many other things. It's not that basketball or football are bad, but when we put those things above Christ they become twisted at their very core.

Do you remember the puzzle board toy that almost every small child tries to solve? The one where you try to put the green triangle piece in the green triangle slot. Then you try to put the purple square in the square slot, and so on and so forth until all the shapes are in their designated slots. We play this game when we start out on life, and no one thinks about it later on down the road. But in reality, the game is a perfect representation of our hearts.

Certain shapes go in certain spots, and certain life experiences should go in the proper area of our heart. If we try to put the square in the circle spot it just won't fit. When we try to put basketball in the spot of our heart that is in the shape of Jesus, it just doesn't fit either. It doesn't satisfy. We can even place reading our Bible or going to church in the spot that is in the shape of Jesus. You can read your Bible every day and go to church every Sunday and still have an extremely unsatisfying life. Our hearts need a *relationship* with Jesus, and that relationship supersedes religion. It is the only thing that truly satisfies, and it does because God designed us to be satisfied in Him alone.

C. S. Lewis once said, "If I find in myself a desire which no experience in this world can satisfy, the most probable explanation is that I was made for another world."[2] And we were made for another world. We were made for a world where we can have an uninhibited relationship with Jesus

Christ in eternity. Lecrae put it another way in his song Outsiders, "Homesick, homeless if I'm on this, cause' my home is somewhere I ain't never been before." Our true home is Heaven. We have never been there but it's exactly where we long to be. This is why we experience feelings of homesickness as believers, and this is why we have a desire which no experience in this material world can satisfy.

In the beginning, there was no sin to get in the way of our relationship with God. However, since the events that took place in the garden, all that has changed. But, the innermost, designed desire to have a relationship with God through Jesus Christ remains in our hearts. Since there are no earthly pleasures, endeavors, good deeds or riches that can satisfy this desire, then it makes sense that God is supposed to be the only thing that can. He is the only piece that fits in the hole of our heart appropriately.

When we try to fit something else in the Jesus-shaped hole of our heart that is not Jesus, then the rough edges of those things can scar our hearts. Just like the rough edges of the square piece can scar the edges of the circle slot in the puzzle board toy. Over a lifetime of cutting our heart with things that were never meant to satisfy it, we can become quite bitter towards our Creator. And if you know anything about scar tissue, then you know that it makes the affected tissue harder than it was before it was damaged. The same is true with our hearts.

The most pronounced cuts and scars that come from trying to be satisfied by the world can come through organized religion—like we mentioned earlier with reading the Bible and going to church. In fact, the people who are usually the most polarized to God are the ones who grew up in a religious home. They went to church, they read their Bible, and they said their prayers. But they did it all out of a "good raising," and not out of a genuine heart that had a relationship with Jesus. It's not always the fault of the parents, though, but often times we as Christian parents can be too overbearing with our religion.

A boy born into a Christian home is not someone born into a relationship with Christ. They are still born into sin, and they will be 100% against God by their very nature. Getting them to do Christian religious tasks makes them no more an actual Christian than making a dog kick a football an actual NFL player. We can pretend all day, but the reality is that our kids need an invasion by Jesus Christ. An invasion that makes them a completely new creature. (Perhaps we have as dramatic of a transformation as going from a dog to an NFL player.)

I'm also not saying we should discourage the reading of the Bible or going to church, because everyone can find Jesus through the Word and talking with His people. But what I am saying is that we shouldn't expect asking our kids to do these types of things to save their souls. They must desperately seek Jesus' presence in their lives, that matters infinitely more than religious routine. If anything, the Devil would love to keep them preoccupied with religious routine so long as they never find the One whom the routines are all about.

But let's get back to the central purpose of this chapter, which was the idea that the world cannot satisfy the deepest desires of our hearts. No amount of religion, money, friends, material things, interpersonal skills, or family can help us find satisfaction in this life. In the end, they will all be disappointing because they are not meant to be satisfying. The only thing that will help you find satisfaction in your life, and therefore help you out of depression, anxiety, lust, doubt, or death, is a relationship with Jesus Christ. This relationship with Him is satisfying because you finally can discover your designed purpose.

He is the eternal and holy Creator of the universe, and for some odd reason He felt compelled to come to this Earth and to die for your sins and to give you purpose. He has come to die for all the times that you put yourself first in your life. When you fell into lust, anxiety, doubt, fear, and depression. Or all the times that you were filled with pride because of the "good deeds" or religious routines that you took part in. He has died for everything you have done, everything you are doing right now, and everything that you will do in the future (that is already recorded in spacetime). He has even died for all the times that you have spoken bad about Him, or told other people that you hated Him. In the end, Jesus is more concerned with spending eternity with you than being bitter towards you for your sins. And let's be honest, we have all done enough stuff against God to disqualify us for heaven. But thankfully God doesn't hold these things against us if we turn to Him and ask for forgiveness.

Speaking of Jesus, He lived out the perfect example for Christians to follow. He obeyed God fully, and He fulfilled God's will for His life in full. We should all pursue this level of commitment. But as we mentioned before, we will not attain this level of commitment and sacrifice on this side of heaven, but we still should pursue it with everything we have. And building off this idea of Jesus being the perfect example, if we are wondering how to find satisfaction, then we should look to Jesus as an example of how *He* found satisfaction. Isaiah 53:11 tells us, "Out of the anguish of his soul he shall see and be satisfied" (ESV). This verse is so powerful because it flips our understanding of satisfaction on its head. Instead of finding satisfaction in comfort, technology, friends, family, money, or good deeds, we find that Jesus found satisfaction in His anguish, pain, and suffering. He found satisfaction in suffering because He was fulfilling God's will for His life, as Isaiah 53:10 tells us, "It was the will of the Lord to crush him" (ESV).

So, if we really want to find satisfaction in this life, then we should find the One who invented the concept and who truly experienced satisfaction. And since Jesus made the human race, it should not be a surprise that He gave us a desire that can only be satisfied by a relationship with Him. Therefore, I beg you to pursue Christ. He is only a conversation away; He is knocking at the door. This means the satisfaction that you seek is very close. The only question is this: Will you open the door?

22

YOU HAVE A BIGGER PURPOSE

There is a passage in Luke chapter sixteen that people don't like to talk about. They don't like to talk about it because Jesus Christ vividly describes Hell. Usually, our untrue stereotypical picture of Jesus is one of an apologetic pushover who is overly nice to everyone all the time. So, it goes against our "Jesus stereotype" to see Him laying down some brutal truth about something as horrible as Hell, and what it must be like.

First, let's establish context.

Jesus was talking to the Pharisees, who were lovers of money. These Pharisees, according to Luke chapter sixteen, were scoffing at Jesus as He discussed that no one can serve two masters. They were mad at Jesus because He was calling them out. He was the king of confrontation, and He was confronting them about their love of money. Essentially, Jesus was telling them that they cannot be dedicated to God *and* money—they must choose between the two.

After establishing this truth, he tells the story of the rich man and the poor man.

I'm going to put this story in today's terms to make it more relatable, but please read Luke sixteen to get a fuller understanding of the context of this passage. But for now, I want you to image that this is Jesus talking today, in the twenty-first century, to the richest business men and women in the United States. The kings and queens of Wall Street; the CEO's of Apple, Google, Microsoft, Exxon Mobile, and any other powerful company that comes to mind.

Therefore, in this passage, the rich man that Jesus would describe would be one from our time period. So, he probably would be wearing the freshest Hugo Boss gear, or perhaps a finely tailored suit from JoS. A. Bank Clothiers. I imagine him wearing one-thousand-dollar sunglasses, and driving a Lamborghini in a tailored black suit.

This rich man lives in a mansion surrounded by a ten-foot-high fence, one in which there is an electronic gate at the front of it. The poor man lays at the rich man's gate—perhaps next to his dumpster—hoping that the rich man will throw away some take-out food for him to scavenge through. This poor and miserable man lives only from the crumbs that fall from the rich man's table. This poor man also has diseases and sores, and the rich man's guard dogs climb through the gate to lick his sores. These dogs are the poor man's only friends. (Mainly because these dogs do not ignore the man due to his poverty. These dogs have more of a generous heart than the rich man.)

Every day, the rich man doesn't even notice the poor man because he is on his phone checking stock prices. He doesn't even notice a man who has lived the majority of his life at the gate of his mansion. All good things seemed to fall right into the rich man's lap, and all bad things seemed to fall into the poor man's.

But one unfortunate day, the poor man dies. Jesus tells us that he is carried away by the angels to Abraham's bosom—which is where faithful people went before Jesus died on the Cross. However, the rich man also dies and is buried. However, the rich man, after living a completely selfish life, goes to Hades. While there, the rich man lifts his eyes in torment, and sees that the poor man, Lazarus, is comforted in Abraham's bosom.

The rich man cries out to Abraham in Luke 16:24, "Father Abraham, have mercy on me, and send Lazarus so that he may dip the tip of his finger in water and cool off my tongue, for I am in agony in this flame" (NASB).

Now, the rich man has become the beggar, the one in want. And the poor man has become rich, living in comfort with Abraham. Abraham's reply in verse twenty-five is that there is a great chasm fixed that prevents anyone from being able to go to Hades and prevents anyone from leaving. Therefore, it is impossible to satisfy his request for water.

The rich man, in complete desperation and realization of the torment of Hell, asks that Abraham may send Lazarus to Earth to warn his five brothers of his pain. Perhaps this will lead them to repentance. But Abraham says, "They have Moses and the Prophets; let them hear them."

The rich man continues to beg, "No, father Abraham, but if someone goes to them from the dead, they will repent!" (NASB).

Abraham's final reply, "If they do not listen to Moses and the Prophets, they will not be persuaded even if someone rises from the dead" (NASB).

This is the reality folks: Hell is a real place. And worst of all, it's an eternal place. People who go there live a tormenting existence of unsatisfaction, pain, and suffering forever. I have five brothers myself, just like the rich man in this passage. All of which I love dearly. My greatest fear—my worst nightmare—is that any of my brothers would spend eternity separated from God. I pray for their salvation because I do not know where all of them stand. It pains me greatly to think that any one of them would go to a place of torment because of their rejection of God's salvation.

But here's the deal: If they were without excuse in the Old Testament because they had the prophets and Moses, how much more will we be without excuse now that we have the Son of God? There is incredible evidence for His miracles, existence, impact, and movement through other believers today.

This sad reality leads us to the question of purpose. If we are without excuse, then we should be spending our life following in Jesus' footsteps. And if we do follow Jesus, then we have a much bigger purpose than living for money like the rich man.

You have the purpose of spreading the gospel. While you shouldn't go around using Hell to scare people into a false repentance, the reality is that without Christ these people will go there when they die. That is the unfortunate truth revealed to us in God's Word, and that reality should motivate us to share the gospel. According to 2nd Peter 3:9, God wishes that none should perish, but that all should reach repentance. We should be motivated by these verses to impact peoples' lives for an eternal purpose.

Mathew 25:46 paints the picture for us, "Then they will go away to eternal punishment, but the righteous to eternal life"

(NIV). The Bible is very clear about the time length of Hell *and* heaven. They are forever according to God, and God is not a liar, nor is He a God of confusion; when he says something is real and eternal, we should pay attention. These are never-ending, literal places of residence for human beings after death.

This fact should resonate in our brains and cause us to reconsider how we operate from a day-to-day basis. There are people that you know personally who are destined for Hell—a real place. If they never confess with their mouth Jesus as Lord, and believe in their heart that God raised Jesus from the dead, then they will not be saved.

In order to lead them to the Cross, we have to follow our purpose. And our purpose is fulfilled most appropriately when we follow our mission. Jesus gave us this mission in Mathew 28:

> All authority in heaven and on earth has been given to me. Therefore go and make disciples of all nations, baptizing them in the name of the Father and of the Son and of the Holy Spirit, and teaching them to obey everything I have commanded you. And surely I am with you always, to the very end of the age. (NIV)

Our instructions are simple: go and make disciples. This is our mission. A component of our *bigger* purpose.

When we have a purpose, we are driven towards the goal that purpose encompasses. In other words, having a good purpose gives us a good goal, and this goal keeps us going. It gives us motivation, aspiration, and most importantly, satisfaction. I believe the degree of satisfaction is reached based on the quality of the goal.

If your goal is to achieve success in this world, then you quite possibly will achieve that goal, but you will never be satisfied. Once achieved, there is nowhere else to climb and you will end up disappointed—as we discussed earlier. When there is nothing else to do, your purpose is erased. However, when your goal is to make disciples and give God glory, there is always work to be done because there will always be one more person that needs a relationship with Jesus Christ, or discipleship, or love, or a friend—all of which are opportunities to give God glory. And when our work on Earth is finished, we will still always have the opportunity to give God glory in Heaven.

Purpose is a microcosm of Christianity. Living purposefully is so reflective of the entirety of the Christian ideals that it may as well be its most basic definition. When you are a Christian, in particular, is when you have a purpose that is higher than yourself. And this is because we have a purpose that was not invented by human minds. You see, when the Creator has given us our purpose, and we follow that purpose, we can rest in full confidence that we are doing with our lives what we should be doing.

When I think of a person who represents what it means to live a purposeful life, there is one person who comes to my mind: Neill Faucett. He is my uncle, and has always been there for me and my family. He is probably the closest thing to a modern-day disciple that I can think of. He is completely sold out to serving Jesus Christ and sharing the gospel. He's the type of person who walks into a room and his face just glows. Almost as if you can see the reflection of Jesus' face in his.

Neill is someone who has spent his entire life serving Jesus Christ in one way or another. And when I look at his family, and the fruit of the Spirit that have been manifested in them, I am blown away. God has worked through my uncle Neill mightily to spread the gospel to his entire family, and has used him to set an example of what a true Christ follower should be like.

His family and hundreds of others will be blessed for generations. Not because my uncle is a great person on his own, but because he has allowed Christ to work through him as a vessel. He has followed Christ's example by making disciples everywhere he goes.

So when my uncle looks back on his life, he has a lot for which to be thankful. To see the people who have come to know the Lord Jesus Christ because he took the time to share the gospel with them. To see his family blessed because of the spiritual leadership and wisdom. To see my family blessed also.

It's truly amazing. It must be an incredible feeling for him to see all that God has done through him.

However, on the other end of the spectrum, there is the person who looks back on their life and has nothing but regret. To the person who has not accepted Jesus Christ as their Lord and Savior, there will be no joy at the end of the tunnel—especially if they are made aware of the consequences of their lifestyle. Because without the Holy Spirit working through you, there will be no spiritual fruit. There will be no spiritual blessings. Only if you are connected with the Holy Spirit will it then work through you to produce good fruit.

My heart breaks for the man who looks back on his life and realizes that he lived it for himself. What a reality of sadness, regret, and depression that must be. You see, at the end of our small earthly existence, there is something so great and long we cannot measure it. And what matters are the lives that have been impacted for that portion—the *eternal* portion. The only way to impact the eternal portion of our existence, though, is to allow the eternal Savior to work through you to save others, because you can do nothing on your own.

When you try to do things on your own is when you will not have love, because you will not have God, and God *is* love.

The lives that have come to know Jesus Christ, the lives that have been saved: this is what we should be concerned with. This is our mission. This is our purpose. Following this mission from our Lord and Savior Jesus Christ gives God immense glory, and that is why we were created. Isaiah 43:7 tells us that we were created for God's glory, so let us choose to live a life that honors and glorifies Him, not ourselves. To do that, we must ask for Jesus to come and live inside of us— to take up residence in our hearts.

At the end of that tunnel is peace, joy, and satisfaction. A life that will be hard, but also one that we will not regret. Second Corinthians 5:15 says, "And he died for all, that those who live might no longer live for themselves but for him who for their sake died and was raised" (ESV). Jesus died for us, the least we can do is live for Him. And if we do not live for Him, at the end of our lives we will discover that we did not live at all.

AFTERWORD

There's always room for one more story, and my story is one that isn't pretty. I know I can talk a big game when I use statistics and Bible references to battle lust, evolution, death, anxiety, or depression; however, when it comes to my own struggles with these issues, it's much harder for me to be bold, open, or vulnerable. To allow myself to be seen as I truly am, a broken and undeserving sinner—the anti-hero. The villain against my own soul. But in order to tell you what goodness God has done in my life, I have to tell you the bad things that used to control me.

I used to be a slave to worldly things (and still am, often) such as anger, lust, discontentment, depression, anxiety, basketball (idolatry), and self-glory. Whatever it was, before I experienced a greater force in my life, I had no power over these areas where the Devil was launching spiritual flaming arrows at me. These arrows were stuck in my heart, cemented deep within, and slowly destroying my life. The flame from the arrows added to the fire of sin that was in my heart. It grew and grew as my passion for lust and self-glory dictated my every thought.

Sin works like a fire, and I think that's why we see a description of Satan firing flaming arrows in Ephesians 6:16. The arrows that Satan fires at us are temptations. Indulgence in them starts because of the initial reception of a flaming arrow from the Evil One. This flame lights a twig, that twig lights a log, and that log lights bigger logs until there is a bon fire. Before you know it, sin can get such a stronghold in your life that it burns out of control. And because it can get so large, it can burn others, even to the point of death.

The bon fire that was my personal sin climaxed with teenage anger, lust, and self-glory problems—like it does for most young men. At the age of fifteen, I was consumed by them. While there were moments I did not succumb to their temptations, it was more often than not that I was defeated in these areas. My spirit was weak, like a weak man that struggles to move railroad ties. There's a slim chance that an extraordinarily weak man can move them, or throw them over his shoulders. For my spiritual life, there was a slim chance that I would ever overcome the sins that dominated my spirit. There was no way that I could extinguish—or at least by my own strength—this bon fire of sin that characterized my life.

Worst of all, I didn't see anything wrong with these sins. With every passing day, my heart indulged in all passions of my flesh that fed the flame, and while significant damage was done to my soul, I didn't really care as long as the flame kept burning. As long as I was entertained. As long as I got whatever it was that I wanted.

The spiritual battle that was going on in my heart, and in my body, was being conquered by the Devil. I had given the reigns over to him, and he was driving the chariot of my heart straight to Hell. Straight to a future where I would be completely distorted in my view of sex. Where I would be an unprepared husband, father, and friend with anger and temperament problems. Where I would become a completely selfish and conceited man who would die alone with many enemies. I was completely and utterly lost. My thoughts (and actions) were influenced more by Satan, than they were by God. And naturally, as sin *is* natural, my mind became distorted, and my actions followed.

However, eventually I was met by a Rock in the road. The Rock of Conviction. I was finally made aware of my sin. It's like my whole life I had been sleeping in a house that was slowly burning. It must have been lit when I was born, as I was born into sin, and the fire of that sin grew as I grew more in alignment with Satan's plan for my destruction. As the Devil launched more and more flaming arrows to the fire, I fell into a deeper and deeper sleep, not knowing that I was so close to being engulfed. Finally, as the fire almost took me, an act of God's grace woke me in the night, and I ran out of that burning house of my own sin and dove into the arms of Christ. And He, with all power and dominion, let rain come down on that house, and extinguished the flames that came from the Devil and inherent sin. Then Christ came to dwell in the house and has been repairing the damage done by the fire ever since.

He has also been building new rooms onto my house. Rooms of love, joy, peace, patience, kindness, goodness, faithfulness, gentleness, and self-control. While each of these rooms has tremendous opportunity for improvement and growth, at least now they are there.

What I mean is this: God saved me. Christ saved me. It was not that I was a person with a tremendous amount of self-control, and that I just decided one evening to live a more righteous life. But it was that at my lowest moment, when I was more indulgent in sin than any other time in my life, that the Holy Spirit convicted me of my sin and Christ offered His hand out to me for salvation. Ever since that moment, God and I have developed a relationship through Christ. And through time spent together, He has slowly healed my wounds as I have slowly learned to let Him heal them.

Time spent together is the key ingredient in our spiritual healing and renewal. If you never spent time with your wife, or your best friend, do you think those relationships would blossom? Do you think that you would know your wife, or your best friend, very deeply? Of course not. This is also true with Christ. If we never spend time with Christ through prayer and reading His word, how do we expect to get to know Him better and to experience change? Time spent together with Christ has resulted in a renewal of my mind, heart, and spirit; it's a daily growth.

It was more than words that I prayed (while there were words prayed); it was true conviction, belief, repentance, and the realization that Jesus Christ was the only One who could save me from my sin. My sin was so great, it was a bon fire, and I had no way to extinguish that flame on my own.

I believe until a person realizes the magnitude of their own sin (that it is an out of control and dangerous fire), they will not see their need for the Savior (the Extinguisher of the flame of sin, and the Repairer of the damage). Therefore, I am thankful now, looking back, that I had such extreme and obvious sin issues. Because if it were not for them, I do not know if I ever would have seen myself for what I really am: a broken sinner in need of the Savior.

Even if you do not have a lust, anger, or pride problem, or any other problem that is more obviously a result of sin, then you must still realize that you are a sinner in need of the Savior. Because even if you think you are in "good standing" on your own accord—if such a thing even existed—you are still spiritually in poor standing with God as a result of simply being born into a world of sin. Ephesians 2:1 gives us a picture of our spiritual lives without Christ, "And you were *dead* [emphasis added] in your trespasses and sins" (ESV).

When something is dead, it is gone, unmoving, and lifeless. For instance, if you died right now, then you would begin to decompose immediately. You would be lifeless. The only way for you to come back to life would be if God resurrected you. I know there are the short-term deaths (or stopped heart beats) of certain persons who are revived because of new technologies—such was the case with my friend, Zade Adams—but they still have nothing on the resurrection power of Jesus. The resurrection power of someone who has been dead for multiple days still resides only with Him; man has nothing on that power.

In this verse (Ephesians 2:1), when we are told that we "were *dead* in our trespasses and sins," we know that victory over this death (which is a spiritual death) is impossible on our own effort. We are spiritually dead in our sins. We cannot resurrect ourselves. We cannot do anything for ourselves to better our inherent condition, or to receive spiritual eternal life. I was spiritually dead before Christ, but God resurrected my life on that day when I was fifteen and I committed my heart to Him. He made me aware of my brokenness, and He came into my heart for a permanent residence. Since then, I have been renewed every day in my thinking.

Whether you are struggling with lust, anger, depression, science, or anxiety, you must realize that you cannot overcome the power of sin and doubt on your own effort. What you will do, without Christ, is trade sins like a card game. You may overcome a lust problem, but in doing so you will take up a pride problem (maybe even a self-righteous problem). Or perhaps you will overcome an anger problem, but then you will soon find yourself being a people-pleaser and eye-pleaser rather than someone who works and loves people out of the sincerity of his or her heart. Whatever it may be, without the surpassing spiritual power of Jesus Christ, you will not defeat sin or make progress, because without Christ you *cannot* defeat spiritual death.

The familiar passage of Ephesians chapter six talks about the armor of God. Particularly in verse eleven, that we should put it on in full to be strong enough to "stand against the schemes of the devil" (ESV). Here is a list of the items that compose the full armor of God:

1. Belt of truth
2. Breastplate of righteousness
3. Shoes prepared with the readiness given by the gospel of peace
4. Shield of faith
5. Helmet of salvation
6. Sword of the Spirit

Do you wear armor to go to a wedding or a war? Indeed, a war, because armor is not for a time a peace. Therefore, the spiritual world is a *warzone*. A war waging in each and every man's heart. Therefore, we must wear armor, and wield a weapon, in order to protect ourselves and fight back in this war.

Belt of Truth

The belt of truth represents Jesus, because He is the truth. Jesus tells us in John 14:6, "I am the way, and the *truth* [my emphasis], and the life. No one comes to the father except through me" (ESV). To better understand this, in the analogy presented to us in Ephesians, think about the function of a belt. In Roman times, it held the sheath for the soldier's sword, as well as holding leather straps that protected the soldier's lower body. It was also at the very center of the soldier's armor. Likewise, at our very core, we should hold fast to the truth that is found in Jesus. The truth of Jesus should be at the center of our spirit. All other truths sprout from the truth of God that is found in Christ.

You cannot even discuss the Old Testament Law without an understanding of the truth of Jesus Christ. Because the Law makes us aware of our sin, and our inability to follow it perfectly. Therefore, without the truth of Christ (who saves us from the punishment that results from the Law), we cannot even have an understanding of the Ten Commandments. Everything in Christianity rests on the foundation that is Christ, He is the chief cornerstone that holds everything together. Just like a belt is the garment that holds the leather straps of protection, and the sheath for the sword. Since the sword of the Spirit is simply God's word, this shows us that we cannot even wield this sword without possessing an understanding of the truth of Jesus. We need the belt of truth (that is Christ), to know how to pull the sword of the Spirit (that is the Bible) out of its sheath, and to apply it appropriately in spiritual warfare.

Breastplate of Righteousness

A breastplate in Roman times was a piece of armor that was used especially for the protection of the heart and other organs in the upper body area. Therefore, a breastplate of righteousness would have to represent some form of spiritual protection. But what do we need protection from spiritually?

Perhaps temptations, anxiety, anger, death, persecution, or fear.

Proverbs 11:4 tells us, "Riches do not profit in the day of wrath, but righteousness delivers from death" (ESV). It is righteousness that is found in Jesus Christ that delivers us from God's wrath; therefore, by wearing this breastplate of Christ's righteousness, we can be protected from God's wrath as well as spiritual attacks from the Devil. Just like a real armored breastplate protects us from physical blows form a sword, so too does a spiritual breastplate protect us from God's wrath (because we are covered in Christ's righteousness) and spiritual attacks from the Devil (because we have God's mark on our armor).

Recall Acts chapter nineteen, when the sons of Sceva attempted to cast out an evil spirit. The evil spirit answered them, "Jesus I know, and Paul I recognize, but who are you?" (ESV). Then the evil spirit overtook them and injured them. So it stands to reason that Demons are aware of Jesus Christ and His great power. They also know those who are saved by Jesus' righteousness and bear the breastplate of righteousness (as Paul is also recognized by the evil spirit). Therefore, without God's breastplate of righteousness, we cannot be protected from evil spirits—as is evident by the evil spirit overtaking the sons of Sceva. However, in Christ, we have this breastplate of righteousness, and we are protected and recognized spiritually, just like Paul.

Shoes Prepared with the Gospel

Shoes are vitally important to anyone who would like to go for a run, hike a mountain, or do anything that may require some tough steps on their journey. Imagine trying to hike a steep rocky mountain with sharp stones protruding at each step. You would be terribly fearful of every step without shoes. You would be forced to focus on the immediate danger, without being focused on the major goal of the journey—perhaps that goal is to climb the highest peak of the Alps. The purpose of shoes, then, is to remove the fear of stepping so that we can focus on what is ahead of us in our journey.

If shoes remove the fear of stepping, then what should (Ephesians 6:15) "as for shoes for your feet, having put on the readiness given by the gospel of peace" do? (ESV). They should remove the fear of stepping in our spiritual journeys.

What it means to put on the shoes with the readiness given by the gospel of peace is this: the gospel brings about absolute peace. Jesus' influence in our heart brings about a peace in our purpose, that if we follow Him we need not be fearful. Second Timothy 1:7, "For God has not given us a spirit of fear, but of power and of love and of a sound mind" (NKJV). God's influence in our life, through the gospel of peace, not only keeps us from fearing the path ahead (and all the spiritual attacks we will face from the Devil), but it also gives us power, love, and a sound mind. All of which we desperately need in our steps to follow Christ to the ends of the Earth; or in our steps to witness to the broken; or in our steps in the battles against sexual immorality, anger, covetousness, depression, suicidal thoughts, or self-righteousness. We desperately need to wear the shoes with "the readiness given by the gospel of peace."

Shield of Faith

The shields of Roman soldiers were known as the "Scutum,"[5] and they were much more than an aesthetic accessory. Weighing in at around twenty-two pounds (or ~10 kilograms),[5] they made for a sturdy piece of equipment that was sure to uphold in the most intense of battles. Unlike the rest of the soldiers' armor, this piece was able to be moved in the direction of oncoming danger. Whether that be a slash by an enemy with a sword, or an arrow sent flying by an archer. Ephesians 6:16 tells us, "In all circumstances take up the shield of faith, with which you can extinguish all the flaming darts of the evil one" (ESV). Spiritually, we must take up this shield, in order to be able to defend ourselves from the attacks of the Devil.

But first, for a deeper understanding of this shield, we must establish what faith is. Many people often ask, "What is faith?" Or perhaps, "Isn't faith blindly believing?"

The Bible defines faith in Hebrews 11:1, "faith is the substance of things hoped for, the evidence of things not seen" (NKJV). So our faith is not something blind (while it is things hoped for), but it is also so much more because we are told that faith is the "substance" of things hoped for. A substance is something tangible, something *real*. Faith is also the "evidence of things" that we cannot see physically. Evidence is defined by the Merriam-Webster dictionary as "An outward sign," or "Something that furnishes proof."[6] Therefore, where are the outward signs of Christ? Where is the tangible nature of faith? Where is the evidence that furnishes *proof* of God?

The physical evidence is obvious. The irrefutable fulfilled prophecy in the Bible, all of the intricately designed biological systems that scream out glory to their Creator, and the amazing accuracy of scripture historically. Take your pick, and if you look deep enough you will find evidence that will lead you in the direction of Christ, and probably to the proof of His existence and resurrection. While these things can lead us to consider Christ, faith is much more than proving Christ through head knowledge. Because faith is substance and evidence that is not seen with our biological eyes. What is not seen with our eyes, but still evidence and substance? The spiritual invasion into our lives by Christ.

Jesus' manifestation in our heart changes us, and this change is spiritual substance and evidence of God. It is

345

something that cannot be seen physically, but it is seen by all through acts of love, service, sacrifice, peacemaking, charity, and kindness.

Ephesians 2:8-9 also tells us that, "For by grace you have been saved through faith; and that not of yourselves, it is the gift of God; not as a result of works, so that no one may boast" (NASB). We are not saved because we are great people, we are saved by grace through faith, and that is a gift from God. And everyone knows that gifts are unearned; therefore, we have an unearned gift from God that is salvation, by grace, and through faith.

When we talk about the shield of faith, we know that shields offer protection for the bearer. So our faith in Jesus Christ has implications in spiritual warfare. We are able to move this shield in the direction of oncoming flaming arrows that are launched by the Devil. Since the Roman shields were also rounded off, arrows could be deflected, or according to Ephesians 6:16, we can "extinguish" these arrows.

In my life, it has been my faith in Jesus Christ that has helped me the most in extinguishing the temptations of the Devil. It has extinguished many of them before they ever took root in my heart. This is because Jesus Christ in my heart dictates my every move. (Whether I prefer Him to rule or not in a situation, He now has great spiritual influence because he has invaded my heart.) Additionally, I have increased faith that

He truly lives inside of me because of this evidence. There is a *substance* to this impact He has had on my life.

Helmet of Salvation

A helmet is obviously used to protect your head, which is supremely important on the battlefield. One strong blow to your head could end your life, or at least ruin your mind. So a helmet of salvation protects our minds in the midst of spiritual battle. With salvation, we are *protected* from God's wrath through the blood of Jesus, but we are also *comforted* by His Spirit. And as a result of these two assets, protection and comfort, we additionally gain mental confidence. These three total assets (protection, comfort, and confidence) guard our minds spiritually.

When I consider the Huddleston family, the helmet of salvation has been immensely protective (by protecting Steven from eternal wrath), it has been comforting (by comforting Steven's family), and it has given us all confidence in the saving power of God's grace. The helmet of salvation should not be underestimated.

Sword of the Spirit

What is a sword used for on the battlefield? To strike, to attack—to play *offense*. All of the other pieces of equipment are really defensive. However, the description of the Word of God being the "sword of the Spirit" really paints a more aggressive picture. So, in spiritual warfare, we should use God's Word for spiritual attacks against the Devil. While the "breastplate of righteousness" gives us comfort and protection and freedom from God's wrath, the "sword of the Spirit" gives us the ability to fight back.

When discussing a sword, I can't help but think about the characteristic sword of Cloud in *Final Fantasy VII*. It's gigantic, super sharp, and bigger than Cloud himself. The same is true with God's Word. Spiritually, the Word is gigantic and powerful, sharper than any two-edged sword (see Hebrews 4:12). It's also bigger than ourselves because it is the Word of our Creator. And according to that same verse, "For the word of God is . . . piercing to the division of soul and of spirit, of joints and of marrow, and discerning the thoughts and intentions of the heart" (ESV). It is powerful, and aggressively pierces into our soul and spirit. Using this spiritual sword is important when defending the Bible, or fighting against spiritual attacks.

For example, my brother Joseph was encountered by some people who were involved with the World Mission Society Church of God. This organization doesn't hold the same beliefs as Christianity; consequently, they tried to convert my brother on the spot. However, my brother was able to refute their distorted views with the use of scripture. He was able to defend God's Word *with* God's Word.

Or, for instance, take our Lord Jesus Christ in the desert in Mathew chapter four. He was tempted by Satan himself, and how did Jesus destroy the Devil's attacks? By slashing back with the Word of God. With each temptation offered from the Devil, our Lord responded by quoting scripture. We should do the same.

Conclusion

To bring our time together to a close, the important thing to note about the armor of God is this: it is *all* about Jesus. The belt of truth—Jesus is truth. The breastplate of righteousness—Jesus' blood makes us righteous. The shoes prepared with the readiness given by the gospel of peace—this is the gospel of Christ. The shield of faith is our faith in Christ Jesus. The helmet of salvation—salvation is given as a free gift because of what Jesus did for us on the Cross. And lastly, the sword of the Spirit, which is the Word of God. His Word tells us the history of how much God loves us through His Son Jesus.

Notice how all of this armor has nothing to do with ourselves. It has everything to do with Jesus Christ. Without Him, we will be worthless in spiritual warfare. Whether you struggle with lust, the presence of bad things happening in our world, the ideas perpetuated by modern scientists, or the effects of depression and suicidal thoughts, all of these battles can be conquered in Christ. He was able to change my mind and heal my heart when it comes to all of these areas. He is able to do that for you also. And I hope you understand that a relationship with Christ is not centered around overcoming addictions, sins, or obstacles. It's about knowing the God of our massive universe in a personal way. As a result of your relationship with Him, you will experience growth and freedom from the things that once held you down.

NOTES

Flaming Arrow #1: Lust

1. Skinner, K. B. (2011). Is Porn Really Destroying 500,000 Marriages Annually? Psychology Today. Retrieved from https://www.psychologytoday.com/blog/inside-porn-addiction/201112/is-porn-really-destroying-500000-marriages-annually

2. Ropelato, J. (2007). Pornography Statistics 2007. Top Ten Reviews. Retrieved from http://www.ministryoftruth.me.uk/wp-content/uploads/2014/03/IFR2007.pdf

3. (2006). "Pornography Statistics." Top Ten Reviews. Retrieved from http://www.toptenreviews.com/internet-pornography-statistics/

4. (2014). Pornography Survey and Statistics. Proven Men Ministries. Retrieved from http://www.provenmen.org/2014pornsurvey/

5. Carter, J. (2013). 9 Things You Should Know About Pornography and the Brain. The Gospel Coalition. Retrieved from https://www.thegospelcoalition.org/article/9-things-you-should-know-about-pornography-and-the-brain

6. Moore, L., & Merritt, J. (2016). Un-ashamed. Nashville, TN: B&H Publishing Group. Nowhere to Run, pp. 29.

7. Jayson, S. (2006). Most Americans have had premarital sex, study finds. USA Today, Health. Retrieved from http://usatoday30.usatoday.com/news/health/2006-12-19-premarital-sex_x.htm

8. Fiorino, D. F., Coury, A. & Phillips, A. G. (1997). "Dynamic Changes in Nucleus Accumbens Dopamine Efflux During the Coolidge Effect in Male Rats." Journal of Neuroscience, 17 (12): 4849–4855

9. Easley, B. (2017). Joy: The Light that Made Me See. Faucett Journal. Retrieved from http://www.faucettjournal.com/articles/joy-the-light-that-made-me-see

10. Lewis, C. S. (2007). *The Complete C.S. Lewis Signature Classics:*

Mere Christianity. HarperSanFrancisco. pp 111
11. Faucett, D. (2017). Parents: The Most Influential People in the World. Faucett Journal. Retrieved from http://www.faucettjournal.com/articles/parents-the-most-influential-people-in-the-world
12. By intimacy I mean a deep and meaningful friendship.

Flaming Arrow #2: Why Do Bad Things Happen?
1. Gaddy, D. (2014). Former Pleasant Valley student killed in single-car crash. The Anniston Star. Retrieved from https://www.annistonstar.com/news/former-pleasant-valley-student-killed-in-single-car-crash/article_48e1b3f0-651d-11e4-8ce4-c7aeb2baa80d.html
2. Penalty. (2017). English Oxford Living Dictionaries. Retrieved from https://en.oxforddictionaries.com/definition/penalty
3. Polarity. (2017). Your Dictionary. Retrieved from http://www.yourdictionary.com/polarity
4. Birth & Death Rates. World Birth and Death Rates. (2011). Retrieved from http://www.ecology.com/birth-death-rates/
5. Sovereignty. (n.d.). Merriam-Webster Dictionary. Retrieved from https://www.merriam-webster.com/dictionary/sovereignty
6. Quotes by Jacques-Marie-Louis Monsabre. (n.d.). AZ Quotes. Retrieved from http://www.azquotes.com/author/29553-Jacques_Marie_Louis_Monsabre

Flaming Arrow #3: Science
1. Orr, James, M.A., D.D. General Editor. (1915). Entry for SANCTIFICATION. International Standard Bible Encyclopedia.
2. Sarfati, J. (2011). Who wrote Isaiah? Creation Ministries International. Retrieved from https://creation.com/isaiah-author-date
3. Kirby, P. (2017). The Histories of Tacitus. Early Christian Writings. Retrieved from

http://www.earlychristianwritings.com/text/annals.html

4. Than, K. (2015). What is Darwin's Theory of Evolution? LiveScience. Retrieved from ://www.livescience.com/474-controversy-evolution-works.html

5. Darwin, C. (1964). The Origin of Species: A Facsimile of the First Edition. Harvard University Press. P.189

6. (2004). Irreducible Complexity: The Challenge to the Darwinian Evolutionary Explanations of many Biochemical Structures. IDEA Center. Retrieved from http://www.ideacenter.org/contentmgr/showdetails.php/id/840

7. Francis, N. R., Sosinsky, G. E., Thomas, D., DeRosier, D. J. (1994). Isolation, characterization and structure of bacterial flagellar motors containing the switch complex. J Mol Biol. 235 (4), 1261–1270

8. Acharya, T. (2013). Bacterial Flagella: Structure, importance and examples of flagellated bacteria. Microbe Online. Retrieved from http://microbeonline.com/bacterial-flagella-structure-importance-and-examples-of-flagellated-bacteria/

9. Wallace, J. W. (2015). Can Evolution Explain the Appearance of Design in Biology? Oklahoma Apologetics Alliance. Retrieved from https://oklahomaapologetics.com/question/can-evolution-explain-the-appearance-of-design-in-biology/

10. Macnab, R. M. (1999). The Bacterial Flagellum: Reversible Rotary Propeller and Type III Export Apparatus. Journal of Bacteriology. Retrieved from http://jb.asm.org/content/181/23/7149.full

11. Behe, M. J. (2006). Darwin's Black Box: The Biochemical Challenge to Evolution. New York: Free Press.

12. (2004). How Big is Our Universe? Office of Space Science, NASA.

13. Britt, R. R. (2004). Universe Measured: We're 156 Billion Light-years Wide! SPACE.com Retrieved from https://web.archive.org/web/20080822013053/http://www.space.com/scienceastronomy/mystery_monday_040524.html \

14. (2015). CODATA Value: proton-electron mass ratio. The

NIST Reference on Constants, Units, and Uncertainty. US National Institute of Standards and Technology. 2014 CODATA recommended values. Retrieved from https://physics.nist.gov/cgi-bin/cuu/Value?mpsme

15. Dorminey, B. (2009). Without the Moon, Would There Be Life on Earth? Scientific American.

16. Lisle, J. (2013). The Solar System: Earth and Moon. Acts & Facts. 42 (10).

17. Mishurov, Yu. N., Zenina, I. A. (1999). Yes, the Sun is located near the corotation circle. Astron. Astrophys. 341, 81-85

18. Deem, R. (2008). The Incredible Design of the Earth and Our Solar System. Evidence for God. Retrieved from http://www.godandscience.org/apologetics/designss.html

19. Sloan, S. (2006). "Earthlike Planets May Be Common." Slice of Scifi. Retrieved from http://www.sliceofscifi.com/2006/09/08/study-earthlike-planets-may-be-common/

20. Sherwin, F. (2006). Is the Universe Crowded with Earthlike Planets? Institute for Creation Research. Retrieved from http://www.icr.org/articles/print/2952/

21. Reliable. (2017). Merriam-Webster Dictionary. Retrieved from https://www.merriam-webster.com/dictionary/reliable

22. Rowitt, S. (n.d.). Carbon-14, Radiometric Dating and Index Fossils. Creation Studies Institute. Retrieved from http://www.creationstudies.org/operationsalt/carbon14.html

23. Keathley, J. H. (2004). The Bible: The Holy Canon of Scripture. Bibliography - The Doctrine of the Written Word. Retrieved from https://bible.org/seriespage/7-bible-holy-canon-scripture

24. Slick, M. (2008). Manuscript evidence for superior New Testament reliability. Christian Apologetics & Research Ministry. Retrieved from https://carm.org/manuscript-evidence

25. (N.d.). Facts about the Bible. MinisterBook. Retrieved from http://ministerbook.com/topics/facts-about-bible/

26. Ally, S. (n.d.). 101 Contradictions in the Bible. Answering

Christianity. Retrieved from http://answering-christianity.com/101_bible_contradictions.htm

27. Deem, R. (2009). Doesn't Genesis One Contradict Genesis Two? Evidence for God. Retrieved from http://www.godandscience.org/apologetics/genesis2.html

28. Chaffey, T. (2010). Do Genesis 1 and 2 Contradict Each Other? Answers in Genesis.

29. Oakes, J. (2008). Why did Jesus get baptized by John if he had no sin? Evidence for Christianity.

30. Lipka, M. (2015). Americans' faith in God may be eroding. Pew Research Center. Retrieved from http://www.pewresearch.org/fact-tank/2015/11/04/americans-faith-in-god-may-be-eroding/

31. Miller, K. (N.d.). Is the Blood Clotting Cascade "Irreducibly Complex?" Retrieved from http://www.millerandlevine.com/km/evol/DI/Clotting.html

32. Geisler, N. L., & Turek, F. (2007). *I Don't Have Enough Faith to Be an Atheist.* Wheaton, IL: Crossway Books. p. 83

33. Heeren, F. (2004). *Show Me God: What the Message From Space is Telling Us About God.* Olathe, KS: Day Star Publications. p. 168

34. Kragh, H. (2009). "Contemporary History of Cosmology and the Controversy over the Multiverse". Annals of Science. 66 (4): 529–551. doi:10.1080/00033790903047725.

35. D.W. Sciama, 'Ist das Universum eigenartig?', in *Vom Urknall zum komplexen Universum,* edited by Jürgen Ehlers, Gerhard Börner and Heinrich Meier (Munich: Piper, 1993), 18394, pp. 19294.

36. To get a more thorough investigation into the expanding nature of the universe, and the evidence that the universe had a beginning, I would suggest that you read *I Don't Have Enough Faith to Be an Atheist* by Norman L. Geisler and Frank Turek.

37. Dawkins, R. (1986). *The Blind Watchmaker.* W.W. Norton & Company, New York, USA. p. 1

38. Other historical sources (among many) for Jesus include: Josephus, The Babylonian Talmud, Pliny the Younger, Mara bar-Serapion.

39. Dawkins, R. (1987). *The Blind Watchmaker*. W.W. Norton & Company, New York, USA. pp. 17-18,116.

40. Luskin, C. (2015). Why the Type III Secretory System Can't Be a Precursor to the Bacteria Flagellum. Evolution News & Science Today. Retrieved from https://evolutionnews.org/2015/07/why_the_type_ii/

41. A quote from The Born-Einstein Letters 1916-55. (n.d.). Retrieved from https://www.goodreads.com/quotes/2669-god-does-not-play-dice-with-the-universe

42. It is important to note that Einstein did not believe in a personal god; however, he was confident that the nature of the universe, and our existence, was no accident.

43. Galatians 5:24 tells us, "And those who belong to Christ Jesus have crucified the flesh with its passions and desires" (ESV). So beyond having the fruit of the Spirit expressed in our lives, we must also have Christ crucify our fleshly passions and desires. Hence, we should have *new* Christ-centered passions and desires.

Flaming Arrow #4: Anxiety

1. (2017). A quote by Benjamin Franklin. Goodreads. Retrieved from http://www.goodreads.com/quotes/21262-tell-me-and-i-forget-teach-me-and-i-may

2. Christian hedonism, a term coined by pastor John Piper in his 1986 book *Desiring God*, means the following: God is most glorified in us when we are most satisfied in Him. Further study on the topic is highly recommended.

Flaming Arrow #5: Depression

1. (N.d.). "Suicide and Depression." All About Depression. Retrieved from http://www.allaboutdepression.com/gen_01.html

2. Lewis, C. S. (2007). *The complete C.S. Lewis Signature classics: Mere Christianity*. San Francisco, CA: HarperSanFrancisco.

3. Sanburn, J. (2012). "Why Suicides Are More Common in Richer Neighborhoods." Time. http://business.time.com/2012/11/08/why-suicides-are-

more-common-in-richer-neighborhoods/
4. (2015). Suicide Statistics. American Foundation for Suicide Prevention. Retrieved from https://afsp.org/about-suicide/suicide-statistics/
5. Benjamin, H. (N.d.). Armor. Victori - The Roman Military – Tools of War. Retrieved from https://romanmilitary.net/tools/armor/
6. Evidence. (n.d.). Retrieved August 2, 2017, from https://www.merriam-webster.com/dictionary/evidence
7. Habeeb, S. [Scott Habeeb]. (2009, July 28). Tom Brady – There has to be more than this [Video file]. Retrieved from https://www.youtube.com/watch?v=4HeLYQaZQW0

Daniel Faucett

INDEX

ABOUT THE AUTHOR

Daniel Faucett lives in Jacksonville, Alabama with his wife Bailey. He has attended both Jacksonville State University and Gadsden State Community College. He has a bachelor's degree in General Science and Education from JSU. He is cofounder of the Steven Huddleston Basketball Camp, and has worked as a counselor at Kanakuk Kamps in Lampe, Missouri; a games director of an Awana program in Rainbow City, Alabama; a volunteer assistant basketball coach; and has worked on undergraduate research at Jacksonville State University.

If you would like to learn more about Daniel or keep up with his newest publications, you can access his website, Faucett Journal, or you can follow his social media pages.

Instagram: @faucettjournal

Twitter: @faucett_journal

Facebook: @faucettjournal

Website: www.faucettjournal.com

92794985R00228

Made in the USA
Lexington, KY
09 July 2018